04/18

Gen

Wedding Bell Blues

Wedding

By MICHAEL BARSON and STEVEN HELLER

Bell Blues

100 Years of Our Great Romance with Marriage

CHRONICLE BOOKS

SAN FRANCISCO

Your Wedding Dress

*Loveliest of the season...
George Jacobson gowns of*

COHAMA RAYON

FORMAL FABRICS

of Celanese* Yarn

*Reg. U. S. Pat. Off.

First Bride: Her rich brocaded gown of Cohama "Desert Moon" rayon satin of Celanese yarn. Subtle flattery in the draped bodice and tiny waistline. About $30. Her halo is edged with braided seed pearls, about $15.

Your local store can get these George Jacobson Originals for you, or write to:
GEORGE JACOBSON, 1400 BROADWAY, NEW YORK CITY . . . ALSO AT:
75 KNEELAND ST.   318 W. ADAMS ST.   912 COMMERCE ST.   850 S. BROADWAY
Boston, Mass.   Chicago, Ill.   Dallas, Texas   Los Angeles, Calif.

Second Bride: Her gown recalls Colonial days. Gown of Cohama "Bridal Tune" rayon satin of Celanese yarn with val lace ruched bodice and sleeves. About $45.00. In bridesmaids' colors, about $25.00. Silk illusion veil, about $20.

To our wives, *Jean Behrend* (the one Michael
tricked into marriage) and *Louise Fili*
(the one doomed to a lifetime with Steve),
who have never once complained about anything —
and who never will, God bless 'em!

FREE
Marriages Perf
With The Purchase
5 gal.
or more GA

Daily

RUNAWAY

BRIDE

LLOYD
HUGHES

MARY
ASTOR

PAUL
HURST

Radio
PICTURES

Acknowledgements

Our gratitude to Archive Photos, Alan Betrock, Joe Burtis, David Feldman, Heidi Fener, Peter Girardi, Joe Koch, Alan Levine, Eric Rachlis, Brian Rose, Kas Schwan, Sarah Shatz, Lloyd Toerpe, Natalie Warady and Lou Valentino, all of whom either made available, or helped locate, some of the vintage materials that illustrate this book.

Library of Congress Cataloging-in-Publication Data available.
ISBN 0-8118-2154-4

Printed in Hong Kong.

Distributed in Canada by Raincoast Books, 8680 Cambie Street, Vancouver, British Columbia V6P 6M9

10 9 8 7 6 5 4 3 2 1

Chronicle Books, 85 Second Street, San Francisco, California 94105

www.chroniclebooks.com

Designed by Heidi Fener / Funny Garbage

All illustrations are from the Michael Barson collection, except those noted as from Archive Photos.

Marriage STORIES

20¢

No. 3

"I've had enough—I'm through!
And I'm not coming back!"

THE LOVE BIRDS—by Catherine Copeland

Contents

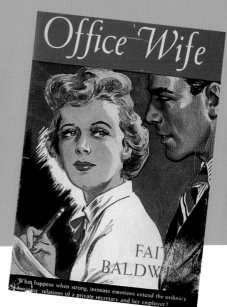

She'd Love To Say "YES" To a Man With a MILLION!

CREST PRODUCTIONS, INC.
presents

CLAUDETTE COLBERT ★ ROBERT YOUNG ★ GEORGE BRENT
in
BRIDE FOR SALE

with MAX BAER · GUS SCHILLING · CHARLES ARNT
Produced by JACK H. SKIRBALL · Directed by WILLIAM D. RUSSELL
Screen Play by BRUCE MANNING and ISLIN AUSTER

Distributed by
RKO RADIO

Oh what a lot of fun this is! Claudette wants a carpet slipper guy for a husband and winds up with a pair of heels! It's positively crazy, but isn't that LOVE?

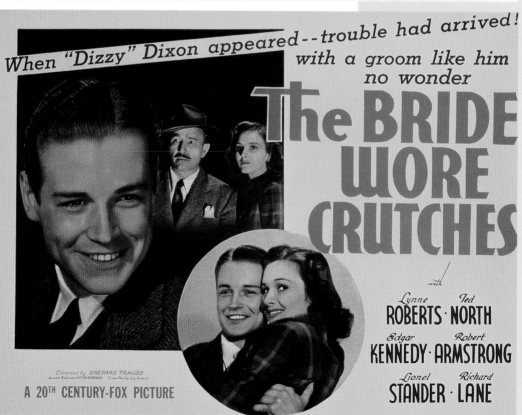

When "Dizzy" Dixon appeared--trouble had arrived!

with a groom like him no wonder

The BRIDE WORE CRUTCHES

with
Lynne ROBERTS · Ted NORTH
Edgar KENNEDY · Robert ARMSTRONG
Lionel STANDER · Richard LANE

Directed by SHEPARD TRAUBE
Associate Producer LUCIEN HUBBARD · Screen Play by Ed Verdier

A 20TH CENTURY-FOX PICTURE

14

He said *"Now!"...*
she said *"Later!"*
...but Mexico City said *"you'll marry Manana!"*

RKO presents

Shirley **TEMPLE**
Franchot **TONE** · Guy **MADISON**
in
Honeymoon

A **WILLIAM KEIGHLEY** Picture

WITH
LINA ROMAY · GENE LOCKHART · CORINNA MURA · GRANT MITCHELL
Produced by WARREN DUFF · Directed by WILLIAM KEIGHLEY
Screen Play by MICHAEL KANIN · Based on a story by VICKI BAUM

George GOBEL
in the happy story of a guy who has but one aim in life...

DIANA DORS
as his favorite target...

What happens to the mouse when the *cheesecake* bites back?

I married a Woman
and they're the best kind!

co-starring
Adolphe MENJOU

with JESSIE ROYCE LANDIS · NITA TALBOT · WILLIAM REDFIELD · STEVE DUNNE   Directed by HAL KANTER · Written by GOODMAN ACE · Produced by WILLIAM BLOOM

15

Prologue

A CENTURY'S WORTH OF FUN FACTS ABOUT MARRIAGE IN AMERICA— AND ITS AFTERMATH

We take it as an article of faith that you, gentle reader, can't possibly make any more sense of the august institution of marriage than we, your faithful authors, both of whom have been married so long that we think of ourselves as husbands first, living organisms second, and men third (when we think at all).

Having admitted as much, let us plunge right into a cold vat of fascinating statistics that help explain why none of us

will comprehend any more about the mysteries of matrimony fifty years hence than we do this very afternoon (which just happens to be Super Bowl Sunday—but so what?). Maybe it's just as well. Maybe some things are best left—unknown.

—Michael Barson married 5.19.84 and Steve Heller married 10.15.83, he thinks

WAS <u>THIS</u> THE MAN SHE HAD MARRIED?

✳✳✳ As of April 1940, there were 28,517,000 married couples living in the United States. By March of 1950, that number had swelled to 36,091,000. And as of March of 1957, the number was 38,940,000, according to the U.S. Bureau of the Census. The state with the highest number of married couples in 1957 was New York, with 3,751,890; the state with the least was Nevada, with a mere 42,415 (perhaps the proximity of Reno and its famously quick-and-painless divorce service accounts for that modest figure).

✳✳✳ The most popular month for marriages in America in 1996 was—you'll never guess!—June, with a rate of 11.2 per 1,000 people in the population, followed in close order by May and August at a rate of 10.7. But, in a shocker, June was overtaken by August as the leader in 1997, with a rate of 11.1 versus 10.6, with September a close third with a rate of 10.5 per thousand. In both 1996 and 1997, the least popular month to get hitched—by a mile—was January, with a feeble 4.6 and 4.9 per 1,000, respectively. (Source: The U.S. National Center for Health Statistics.)

✳✳✳ In 1997, approximately 2,380,000 couples got married in the United States, a slight increase over 1996's total of 2,340,000. The total number of divorces in 1997 fell just an iota, from nearly 1,200,000 couples in 1996 to 1,115,000. By our calculations, that indicates that about half of the marriages commencing these days could be expected to work out—for a while, anyway.

Archive Photos

✳✳✳ According to the U.S. National Center for Health Statistics, there were more marriages in America in 1920—a rate of 12 per 1,000 in the population—than there were in 1925 (10.3 per thousand), 1930 (a mere 9.2—chalk it up to the Great Depression!), or 1935 (10.4). But by 1940, the rate had climbed to 12.1. Ten years later, the rate had fallen to 11.1, and it kept falling for the next fifteen years—to 9.3 in 1955, 8.5 in 1960, and 9.3 in 1965. From 1970 through 1985, the rate was fairly stable, remaining around 10 marriages per 1,000 people, but lately the rate has slowly declined, from 9.8 in 1990 to just 8.6 per 1,000 Americans in 1996 and 8.9 in 1997.

✳✳✳ Since 1920, the rate of divorces in America has fluctuated dramatically. From 1920 through 1935, the rate was relatively stable at the modest figure of 1.5 to 1.7 divorces for each 1,000 Americans. In 1940, the figure jumped slightly, to 2 per 1,000, and by 1945, divorces had reached the highest percentage to date, 3.5 divorces per 1,000 Americans—a factor of homefront trauma from World War II, perhaps? From 1950 through 1965, the rate dropped back below 3. But by 1970, the figure of 3.5 per 1,000 was reached again, and thereafter the rate steadily climbed: from 4.8 in 1975 to an all-time high of 5.3 in 1979 (probably the Jimmy Carter factor—or was it the lure of Disco?) to 5 in 1985. But since those dark days, the rate of divorces in America has fallen steadily—for 1996 and 1997 it was 4.3, the lowest rates in over twenty years. Encouraging news for all matrimony fans!

✳✳✳ On the other hand, as of 1998, America's divorce rate was still the highest in the world.

✳✳✳ In 1997 there were 11,100,000 divorced women living in America, compared to only 8,200,000 divorced men. Seem impossible? Not when you factor in that women are less likely than men to remarry following a divorce (and consider, too, the longevity factor, which falls in favor of women by quite a margin). Those 19.3 million divorcees accounted for 9.9 per-

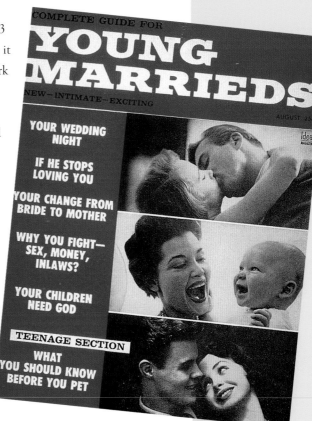

COMPLETE GUIDE FOR
YOUNG MARRIEDS
NEW—INTIMATE—EXCITING
AUGUST 25¢
Ideal MAGAZINE

YOUR WEDDING NIGHT
IF HE STOPS LOVING YOU
YOUR CHANGE FROM BRIDE TO MOTHER
WHY YOU FIGHT—SEX, MONEY, INLAWS?
YOUR CHILDREN NEED GOD
TEENAGE SECTION
WHAT YOU SHOULD KNOW BEFORE YOU PET

cent of the total U.S. adult population in 1997, a slightly higher ratio than the year before.

✳✳✳ In New York State, between 1967 and 1972, the incidence of divorce increased 1,000%.

✳✳✳ According to a *Time*/CNN poll of 1,017 Americans taken on May 7 and 8, 1998, 64% believed that people should be required to take a marriage-education course before they can obtain a marriage license; 61% believed that couples with children should face stricter requirements for getting a divorce; and 50% felt divorce laws should be stricter for couples in general. On the other hand, 59% felt that it was not the province of the government to dictate those stricter laws.

✳✳✳ Surprisingly, the median age for first marriage for both men and women has fluctuated very little since 1890, when the U.S. Bureau of the Census began compiling its information. For women, the median ages have ranged from a low of 20.3 in both 1950 and 1960 to an all-time high of 25 during 1997. For men, the tale is quite similar, with a low median age of 22.8 in both 1950 and 1960 and highs of 26.9 posted in 1995 and 26.8 in 1997 (not enormously different from the 26.1 median for men recorded way back in 1890).

✳✳✳ Is it true that unmarried women outnumber unmarried men? Not during the peak years for marriage, according to *The New York Times 1999 Almanac*. Using 1997 for data, it was revealed that, between the ages of 18 and 25, there actually were 113 unmarried men for every 100 unmarried women. The surplus is even more pronounced for the 25 to 34 age group, with 126 unmarried men for every 100 women. From age 35 to 44, unmarried men still have the edge at 104 to 100, but after that, pickings for women in search of marriage partners do indeed become slim. For the 45 to 64 age group, unmarried women outnumber unmarried men 100 to 69, and for ages 65 and over, the ratio is a frightening 100 women for every 32 unmarried men. (This is where the longevity of women vs. men really starts to work against them.)

✳✳✳ According to a 1998 *USA Today* "Snapshot" based on a study conducted by Moet Matrimonial Matrix, wedding costs in the United States have risen significantly since 1993, with 1997 showing an increase of almost 8%. Hey— it's still the best deal in town for your entertainment dollar!

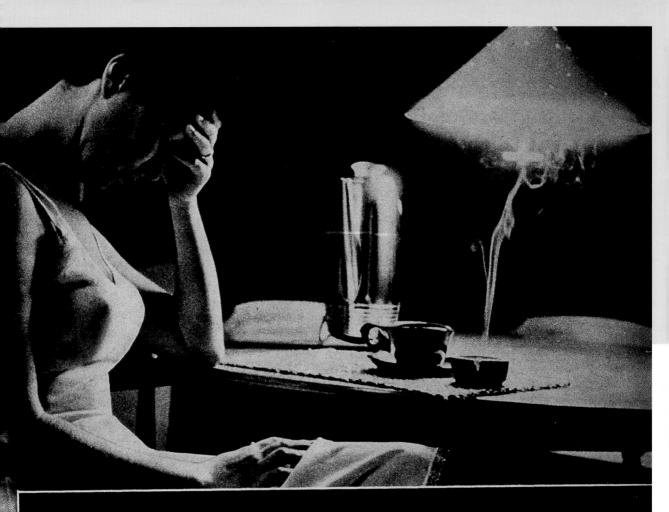

RUNAWAY HUSBANDS

A NATIONAL EPIDEMIC

Words of Wit, Wisdom, and Remorse

1

THE SAGES OF THE AGES ON MARRIAGE

You think you're mixed-up about the ins and outs of wedlock? (Wedlock—now, there's a compound noun that carries certain implications!) So it has always been for the great minds of each age of humankind. If four thousand years of civilization's Alpha thinkers and philosophers couldn't figure out what marriage means, what chance do we have of cracking the code? So be our guest—jump in, and drink from the fountain of wisdom that follows. And then, after quaffing this heady brew, be prepared to get *really* confused!

WEDDING BELLS

(ARE BREAKING UP THAT OLD GANG OF MINE)

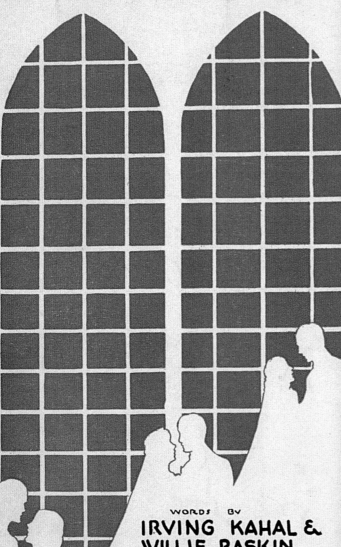

WORDS BY
IRVING KAHAL &
WILLIE RASKIN
MUSIC BY
SAMMY FAIN

With Ukulele Arrangement

WATERSON-
BERLIN
&
SNYDER CO.
Music Publishers
Strand Theatre Bldg
Broadway at 47th St.
NEW YORK

MADE IN USA

258

CITY CLERK
MARRIAGE
LICENSE BUREAU

It is better to marry than to burn.

—Corinthians

Whoso findeth a wife findeth a good thing.

—*Proverbs*, 18:22

A virtuous woman is a crown to her husband.

—*Proverbs*, 12:4

By all means marry; if you get a good wife, you'll be happy.
If you get a bad one, you'll become a philosopher.

—Socrates

Two days are the best of a man's wedded life
The days when he marries and buries his wife.

—Hipponax (Sixth century B.C.)

The bachelor is a peacock, the engaged man a lion,
the married man a jackass.

—German proverb

The comfortable estate of widowhood is the only hope that keep's
up a wife's spirits.

—John Gay, *The Beggar's Opera*

Never marry a widow unless her first husband was hanged.

—Old English Proverb

Marriage has many pains, but celibacy has no pleasure.

—Samuel Johnson, *Rasselas*

One fool at least in every married couple.

—Henry Fielding, *Amelia*

I Spelled Marriage—"M·I·R·A·G·E"

Listen to this
wife's story of marriage
happiness rediscovered

❀ Composed that monstrous animal
a husband and wife.

—Henry Fielding, *Tom Jones*

❀ They took from me my wife, and to
save trouble I wed again, and made the error
double.

—John Clare, *The Exile*

❀ Wedlock, a padlock.

—Old English Proverb

❀ There is but one hour a day between
a good housewife and a bad one.

—Old English proverb

❀ Woe to the house where the hen
crows and the rooster keeps still.

—Spanish proverb

❀ Wives rarely fuss about their beauty
To guarantee their mate's affection.

—Molière, *The School for Wives*

❀ One was never married, and that's his hell;
another is, and that's his plague.

—Robert Burton, *The Anatomy of Melancholy*

❀ Oh! How many torments lie in the small circle
of a wedding-ring!

—Colley Cibber, *The Double Gallant*

❀ A light wife doth make a heavy husband.

—Shakespeare, *The Merchant of Venice*

❀ Many a good hanging prevents a bad marriage.

—Shakespeare, *Twelfth Night*

❀ We will have no more marriages.

—Shakespeare, *Hamlet*

❀ A young man married is a man that's marred.

—Shakespeare, *All's Well That Ends Well*

❀ Men in single state should tarry;
While women, I suggest, should marry.

—Samuel Hoffenstein

❀ Though women are angels, yet wedlock's the devil.

—Lord Byron

❀ In matrimony, to hesitate is sometimes to be saved.

—Samuel Butler

❀ Well-married, a man is winged
—ill-matched, he is shackled.

—Henry Ward Beecher

❀ Marriage is a feast where the grace is sometimes better than the dinner.

—Charles Caleb Cotton, *Lacon*

❀ Marriage is like life in this—that it is a field of battle, and not a bed of roses.

—Robert Louis Stevenson

❀ Times are changed with him who marries; there are no more by-path meadows, where you may innocently linger, but the road lies long and straight and dusty to the grave.

—Robert Louis Stevenson

❀ Strange to say what delight we married people have to see these poor fools decoyed into our condition.

—Samuel Pepys

❀ Have you not heard
When a man marries, dies, or turns Hindoo,
His best friends hear no more of him?

—Percy Bysshe Shelley, *Letter to Maria Gisborne*

❀ As the husband is, the wife is: thou art mated
   with a clown,
And the grossness of his nature will have weight
   to drag thee down.
He will hold thee, when his passion shall have
   spent its novel force,
Something better than a dog, a little dearer than his horse.

—Alfred, Lord Tennyson, *Locksley Hall*

❀ Keep your eyes wide open before marriage, half shut
afterwards.

—Benjamin Franklin

❀ The men that women marry, and why they marry them,
will always be a mystery to the world.

—Henry Wadsworth Longfellow

❀ Divorce is of probably the same date
as marriage. I believe, however, that
marriage is some weeks more ancient.

—Voltaire

❀ Marriage is a science.

—Honore de Balzac

❀ It is a truth universally acknowl-
edged that a single man in possesssion
of a good fortune must be in want
of a wife.

—Jane Austen, opening
line of *Pride and Prejudice*

In This Issue
BRIDES OF 1938

❀ Marriage is a lottery in which men stake their liberty and women their happiness.

—Madame de Rieux

❀ Every woman should marry — and no man.

—Benjamin Disraeli

❀ It is most unwise for people in love to marry.

—George Bernard Shaw

❀ Men marry because they are tired, women because they are curious; both are disappointed.

—Oscar Wilde

❀ Don't wish me happiness . . . wish me courage and strength and a sense of humor — I will need them all.

—Anne Morrow Lindbergh (just before her marriage)

❀ How marriage ruins a man. It's as demoralizing as cigarettes, and far more expensive.

—Oscar Wilde, *Lady Windemere's Fan*

❀ If couples did not live together, happy marriages would be more frequent.

—Friedrich Wilhelm Nietzsche, *Human, All Too Human*

❀ The only really happy folk are married women and single men.

—H. L. Mencken

✿ If you want to sacrifice the admiration of many men for the criticism of one, go ahead, get married.

—Katharine Hepburn

✿ Marriage halves our griefs, doubles our joys, and quadruples our expenses.

—Vincent Lean

✿ Separate bedrooms and separate bathrooms.

—Bette Davis

✿ To keep your marriage brimming
   With love in the loving cup,
   Whenever you're wrong, admit it,
   Whenever you're right, shut up.

—Ogden Nash

✿ I lost a good secretary and found a lousy cook.

—Fiorella H. La Guardia

✿ I personally adore marriage . . .
I even cry at weddings, especially my own.

—Zsa Zsa Gabor

✿ A man in love is incomplete until he's married.
Then he's finished.

—Zsa Zsa Gabor

✿ Marriage is the death of hope.

—Woody Allen

Professor Harold Bloom Presents the Five Happiest Marriages in Shakespeare:

1) **THE MACBETHS**, in *Macbeth.*

2) **KING CLAUDIUS AND GERTRUDE**, in *Hamlet.*

3) **PETRUCHIO AND KATE**, in *The Taming of the Shrew.*

4) **CAESAR AND CALPURNIA**, in *Julius Caesar.*

5) **BRUTUS AND PORTIA**, in *Julius Caesar.*

COLUMBIA PICTURES PRESENTS

...ETH RICHARD
...R BURTON

...BURTON-ZEFFIRELLI PRODUCTION OF

...G OF THE SHREW

...ERN · ALFRED LYNCH · ALAN WEBB with VICTOR SPINETTI
Screenplay by PAUL DEHN, SUSO CECCHI DAMICO, FRANCO ZEFFIRELLI *
*(with acknowledgements to William Shakespeare without whom they would have been at a loss for words)
...cted by FRANCO ZEFFIRELLI · A ROYAL FILMS INTERNATIONAL/F.A.I. PRODUCTION
Original soundtrack recording available as an RCA Victor Red Seal Album

Expertise from a Century's Worth of Marriage Manuals

THROUGH THE YEARS WITH A WHOLE BUNCH OF KNOW-IT-ALLS

TALKS ON NATURE: *A True Marriage Guide* by J. H. Greer, M.D. (1888) ❋ Let no married lovers think of habitually occupying the same bed. It can do no good . . . What one may gain in vitality the other loses . . . Aside, and above all other reasons, is the one that separate beds will in great measure help overcome sexual excesses. The close bodily contact under a common bed-clothing is a constant provocation to amorous ideas and sensations. It is the purely sensual that needs to be put to one side that the spiritual may have a chance for growth.

WEDLOCK: *Or, the Right Relations of the Sexes, Disclosing the Laws of Conjugal Selection, and Showing Who May, and Who May Not Marry* by S. R. Wells (1888) ❋ A Word to Husbands: Make allowance for

Sex and Marriage Problems

from the intimate records of a psychoanalyst

as told to
E. B. TAYLOR

The Case of ... The Girl Who Couldn't Say No • The Frigid Wife • The Strange Love Triangle • The Wife Who Feared Children • The Girl Who Couldn't Say Yes • The Man Who Hated His Son • The Ugly Duckling • The Husband Stealer • The Jealous Woman • The Husband Who Had To Have Affairs

your wife's share of the great inheritance of human nature. Do not expect her to smile in unmoved serenity when children are ungovernable, servants are in high rebellion, and husband comes home cross and hungry. If she is a little petulant, do not bang doors by way of soothing her temper . . .

Because a man has married a woman, does it necessarily follow that thenceforward he is exonerated from all the duties of ordinary civility toward her? By all the wedding rings in Christendom, *no*!

SEXOLOGY by Professor Wm. H. Walling, A.M., M.D. (Philadelphia: Puritan Publishing Co., 1907) ❊ The gratification of their own lust—we cannot term it pleasure—is, with the majority of men, the leading idea connected with the marriage bed—to their shame be it spoken. A woman of much social and intellectual distinction said, not long ago, "When my husband closes the door of our apartments at night, he is no longer a man, he is a monster!" . . . For a woman subjected to the most hellish tortures under the form of "marital rights," there would seem to be, literally, no redress either in "Church or State." Religion replies to such a one, "Your duty to your husband is submission," while the Civil Code utterly ignores her complaint.

From the Table of Contents to WHAT A YOUNG HUSBAND OUGHT TO KNOW by Sylvanus Stall, D.D. (1907) ❊ CHAPTER VI: MARITAL MODERATION Twofold nature of love. —Rooted in the physical, flowers in the spiritual. —Lust often miscalled love. —Three theories concerning the marital relation. —Unrestrained indulgence for men. —For procreation only. —As an expression of affection and for mutual endearment. —The perpetuity of the race and the highest good of the individual consistent. —What is marital moderation?; difficulty in defining. —Strong words from Mrs. E. B. Duffy. —Marital moderation vs. conjugal debauchery. —Degrading effects of sexual excess. —The wishes of the wife always to be respected. —Stimulating food, books, pictures, etc. —Importance of single beds and separate apartments. —Manly mastery worth all it costs. —The struggle not endless.

WHAT A YOUNG WIFE OUGHT TO KNOW by Mrs. Emma Angell Drake, M.D. (1908) ❖ There is a vast amount of vital force used in the production and expenditure of the seminal fluid. Wasted as the incontinence of so many lives allows it to be, and prostituted to the simple gratification of fleshy desire, it weakens and depraves. Conserved as a legitimate control demands it to be, it adds so much, and more to the mental and moral force of the man, because it lifts him to a higher plane of being, and gives to the mental and moral the vital force otherwise wasted.

SELF KNOWLEDGE AND GUIDE TO SEX INSTRUCTION: *Vital Facts of Life for All Ages* by Professor T. W. Shannon, A.M. (1913) ❖

>> *Should husband and wife sleep together or in separate beds?* — In many cases, owing to lack of self-control, it would be better for them to sleep in separate beds.

>> *How frequently should husband and wife have sexual relations?* — There is no more necessity for sex gratification in the married life than in the single. Those who have this self-control will be able to avoid all dangers, sins, and diseases incident [sic] to a lack of control . . . The other theory is that of physical necessity. Among the married it means legal prostitution, leads to marital excess, poor health of parents, loss of vitality, puny, scrawny, short-lived children, and to "race suicide."

>> *Are women as passionate as men?* — Many women do not feel any sexual excitement whatever, others only to a limited degree . . . Most normal women seek sexual gratification to please their husbands or out of a desire for motherhood.

>> *At what periods during the month is a wife most likely to become a mother?* — Just before or after the menses.

NATURE'S SECRETS REVEALED: *Scientific Knowledge of the Laws of Sex Life and Heredity, or Eugenics* by Professor T. W. Shannon, A.M. (1914) ❖ The married man who thinks that, because he is a married man, he can commit no excess, no matter how often the sexual act is repeated, will suffer as certainly and as seriously as the debauchee who acts on the same principle in his indulgences . . . and from his not taking those precautions and following those rules which a career of vice is apt to teach a man.

The best mothers, wives and managers of households know little or nothing of the sexual pleasure. Love of home, children and domestic duties are the only passions they feel. As a rule, the modest woman submits to her husband, but only to please him; and, but for the desire of maternity, would far rather be relieved from his attentions.

MARRIED LOVE: *A New Contribution to the Solution of Sex Difficulties* by Marie Carmichael Stopes (New York: Eugenics Publishing Co., 1918, 1927, 1931) ❋ My law of Periodocity of Recurrence of desire in women it is possible to represent graphically as a curved line; a succession of crests and hollows as in all wave lines . . . Woman is so sensitive and responsive an instrument, and so liable in our modern civilized world to be influenced by innumerable sets of stimuli, that it is perhaps scarcely surprising that the deep, underlying waves of her primitive sex-tides have been obscured, and entangled so that their regular sequence has been masked in the choppy turmoil of her sea.

SANE SEX LIFE AND SANE SEX LIVING by H. W. Long, M.D. (Boston: Richard G. Badger, 1919) ["Sold only to members of the recognized professions"] ❋ The beautiful and delicate flowers of married love need to be watched and tended with the most skillful care, continually, by both husband and wife . . . Let married people understand that the key to marital happiness is to keep on "courting" each other. Indeed, to make courting continually grow to more and more. During the whole extent of married life, never neglect, much less forget to be lovers, and to show, by all your acts, that you are lovers, and great shall be your reward. Don't ask how to do this! You know how, well enough. Do it!

FACTS ABOUT MARRIAGE EVERY YOUNG MAN & WOMAN SHOULD KNOW by S. Dana Hubbard, M.D. (1922) ❋ On your wedding night, be tender, considerate, and appreciate that the little wife has had a day of excitement and nervous and physical strain. Your wife and you are alone. She is absolutely yours and for the first time is entirely in your power. At your mercy. If you shock or disgust her by precipitancy or over eagerness, or zeal, appreciate it may be the undoing of your wedded bliss and joy. You may regret it the balance of your life . . . The honeymoon is often one nightly repetition of legalized prostitution sinking the pure, the high and the holy into the low and debasting [sic] lust of over excited passion.

WHAT IS WRONG WITH MARRIAGE by G. V. Hamilton, M.D., and Kenneth Macgowan (New York: Charles Boni, 1929) ❋ When did the [one hundred husbands surveyed] begin to find something wrong—seriously wrong—with their marriages? [One question] read: "If by some miracle you could press a button and find that you had never been married to your wife, would you press that button?". . . Sixty-six men gave immediate and unqualified answers of "No," eight more said "No" but added qualifications, and five were uncertain. There were only seventeen who more or less definitely would have ended their marriages . . . Thus the husbands grow better and better satisfied with their marriages—far better satisfied than the examiner can convince himself they should be.

MARRIAGE AND MORALS by Bertrand Russell (New York: Liveright, 1929) ✳ Marriage is for women the commonest mode of livelihood, and the total amount of undesired sex endured by women is probably greater in marriage than in prostitution.

THE REMAKING OF MARRIAGE by Poul Bjerre, M.D. (New York: Macmillan, 1931) ✳ It is a dangerous period when the wife begins to draw comparisons and to look upon her partner as an obstruction to winning that perfect creature she might possibly have met provided this one had not crossed her path and barred the way . . . Everything the husband might give is nothing compared with that which the other, the right one, would have been able to give.

MARRY OR BURN by George Ryley Scott (New York: Greenberg, 1931) ✳ Seeing that a man selects his partner for life with much less care than he selects a residence, a horse, or even a dog, it is not surprising that he meets with big and painful surprises when the mask slips . . . Queerly enough, although the disillusionment that comes to each partner after marriage breeds discontent with the union and irritation with the other partner, it rarely, if ever, prevents a repetition of the disease.

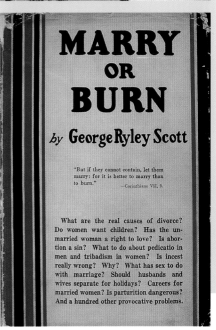

THE TORCH OF LIFE by Frederick M. Rossiter, B.S., M.D. (New York: Eugenics Publishing Co., 1932) ✳ The abundant precoital fluid supplied by the woman prepatory to and during union, and even at the orgasm, is of no vital importance; and for this reason women can stand excessive coitus far better than men, and with less impairment of their vital resources. This is a point for a well-sexed woman, or one who is oversexed, to bear in mind; for her husband may not be able to keep up with her without reducing his vitality . . . A man is in better vigor if his system absorbs all the extra semen, than when it is lost, or spent in wasteful extravagance.

FROM FRIENDSHIP TO MARRIAGE by Roy A. Burkhart, M.D., Ph.D. (1937) ❋ A relatively small percentage of couples who have had premarital intercourse do later attain married happiness. Those who remain continent until marriage have markedly better chances of attaining happiness . . . Of the one thousand married couples I studied by means of a questionaire . . . most of the happy group postponed intimacy even though they were engaged longer and "dated" longer than those of the other group.

MARRIAGE by Leon Blum (Philadelphia: Lippincott, 1937; translated from the French) ❋ But women are becoming every day less reconciled to obedience and self-sacrifice . . . What a singular state is marriage, which weighs more heavily on frankness than it does on falsehood, on virtue than it does on vice! The most pitiful victims of present-day marriage are the women who adhere to its terms most loyally.

From the Preface to the eleventh printing of **SEX LIFE IN MARRIAGE** by Oliver M. Butterfield (New York: Emerson, 1937, 1947) ❋ This book was written for those, married or contemplating marriage, who wish to live wholesome and happy lives, and who realize they need detailed and reliable information to do so. Recent studies indicate that when both partners have a fund of sound sex information, the prospects for a successful marriage are greatly increased . . . The material included here is based upon many years of first-hand experience as a marriage counselor. [This] book attempts to show how marriage may be made a more successful and attractive state than has heretofore been generally achieved.

THE POWER TO LOVE: *A Doctor's Guide to Ideal Marriage Relationship* by Edwin W. Hirsch, B.S., M.D. (New York: Garden City Publishing, 1934, 1938) ❋ Body movement in the display of the grand passion has until recently been tabooed. Now wives are beginning to realize that rotation of their hips during the sexual act is a normal reaction to sexual stimulation. It is now considered perfectly normal and ethical for the wife to undulate her pelvis rhythmically during bodily communion. In fact, it has never been unnatural; it is only the thinking of certain "upright" ones that has made it appear so.

SECRETS OF LOVE AND MARRIAGE by James Parker Hendry and Edward Podolsky, M.D. (New York: Herald Publishing, 1933, 1939) ✻ THE OVER-DEMONSTRATIVE HUSBAND: There is another grave danger in such a marriage as I am describing. Any husband can carry his courtship to his wife to the point where he ceases to be interesting and becomes a nuisance. If the wife resents the constant fondling of a husband overly amorous, she is quite likely to turn to a man who is more reserved in his manner. No woman wants to be mauled on every occasion . . . No man would want to be continually pawed and petted and cuddled, so why should a woman?

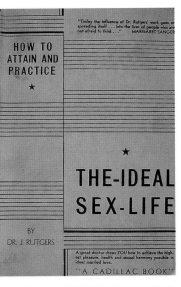

HOW TO ATTAIN AND PRACTICE THE IDEAL SEX LIFE by Dr. J. Rutgers (New York: Cadillac Publishing, 1940) ✻ *Aim of the Author:* To educate men and women in the clearest, simplest language how to overcome their individual sexual problems. To point out the pitfalls of the ignorance of sex knowledge—how to avoid them, how to remedy them. To help you realize the ideal sex life and thereby do away with the setbacks of many, many marriages . . . misery, poor health, and failure!

THE WAY OF A MAN WITH A MAID by Oscar Lowry (1940) ✻ If the boy has been taught the sacredness of sex relationships since childhood, he will have been brought to realize the seriousness of wedded life, and the importance of keeping himself physically and morally clean in anticipation of a happy wedding day . . . Fortunate indeed is that young man who can bring to the bridal chamber a strong, clean body, untainted by disease, and a consciousness that his life has been as pure and chaste as that of the one whom he has chosen to be his life companion . . . No man was ever the worse for continence, and that regardless of what any infidel college or university professor may teach the unsuspecting youth of our nation.

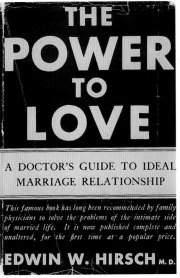

STRANGE CUSTOMS OF COURTSHIP AND MARRIAGE by William J. Fielding (New York: Garden City, 1942, 1949) ✻ Companionate Marriage — During the latter half of the 1920s a nation-wide controversy took place in the United States over the proposal termed companionate marriage, advanced by Judge Ben B. Lindsey of Denver, Colorado. In brief, [this] is a legal marriage entered into by two people with the intention of having no children for an indefinite period, and in which neither would assume financial responsibility for the other.

LOVE WITHOUT FEAR: *How to Achieve Sex Happiness in Marriage* by Eustace Chesser, M.D. (New York: Roy Publishers, 1947) ❊ Prince Charming holds many married women in bondage. They compare their very human, and therefore ordinary, husbands, with the dream figure of the handsome prince, and feel badly let down. Why is not the husband all that the good prince has been for so many years? Why is not this husband of reality as perfect as the dream picture?

Men are sometimes enslaved by a fairy princess in exactly the same way . . . Alas, life is not at all like that. Those who realize this truth will be the happier for the knowledge!

SEX AND MARRIAGE PROBLEMS: *From the Intimate Records of a Psychoanalyst* as told to E. B. Taylor (New York: Hillman Periodicals, 1948) ❊ I want you to think over what I've said, Eve, before you condemn me as a doctor, as a psychiatrist. The first constructive step you ever took was to submit to psychoanalysis, Eve. And the second step I want you to take is to go to that dude ranch.

From the Foreword by Robert B. Greenblatt, M.D., to **SEXUAL FEELING IN MARRIED MEN AND WOMEN** by G. Lombard Kelly, M.D. (New York: Pocket Books, 1951) ❊ To learn about the sexual urge and to understand it is not to demean ourselves . . . Perhaps for some husband and wife who reads this little opus the ways of a man and a maid may be made more pleasant, and the impulses that bring them together will not be attended by fears, selfishness and anguish. Knowledge and understanding will add dignity, honor and beauty to their most intimate of functions.

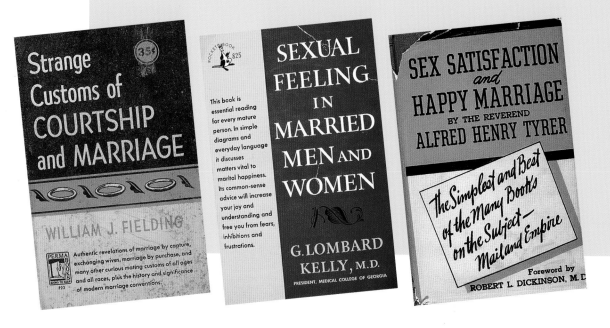

SEX SATISFACTION AND HAPPY MARRIAGE by the Reverend Alfred Henry Tyrer (New York: Emerson Books, 1951, 1958) ❊ Young couples need to live together, with no call for any divided allegiance. It is an imposition for any husband to bring his mother into his wife's home . . . That kingdom belongs to the wife he has taken unto himself. It is an imposition for any wife tacitly to assume that her husband married her family as well as herself.

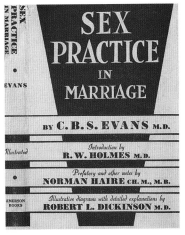

SEX PRACTICE IN MARRIAGE by C. B. S. Evans, M.D. (New York: Emerson Books, 1951) ❊ A last bit of advice, which pertains to all matters of married life, may be offered. Never sleep over a difference! Smooth out the difficulties if you have to stay awake until dawn. One of the most harmful tactics a husband or wife can employ is to close up like a clam and refuse to talk the disputed matter through. It is indulged in small spoiled children and large spoiled adults. It is the old story of "I won't play." Good sportsmanship and a sense of humor are indispensible to happiness in marriage.

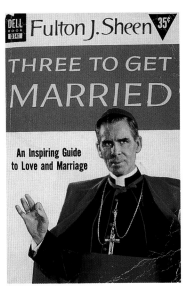

THREE TO GET MARRIED: *An Inspiring Guide to Love and Marriage* by the Most Reverend Fulton J. Sheen (New York: Dell, 1951) ❊ The world is full of people who "give up" instead of going forward in a marriage. The Christian doctrine on the unbreakable quality of marriage is aimed at character making. It wants captains to stay on deck during a storm and not jump overboard. Too many are now deserting their ships. As the French proverb puts it, "Divorce is the sacrament of adultery!" . . . To read some modern books, one would think that the biggest problem in marriage was that of being sexually adjusted.

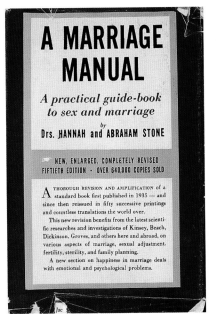

A MARRIAGE MANUAL: *A Practical Guide-Book to Sex and Marriage* by Drs. Hannah and Abraham Stone (New York: Simon & Schuster, 1935, 1952; revised fiftieth edition) ❊ *Can a husband tell when his wife has been sufficiently aroused and is ready for sexual union?* Yes, he can often learn to recognize the emotional and physical signs of the degree of the wife's arousal. Where there is a mutual frankness and absence of inhibitions, it will not be difficult for the husband and wife to sense each other's reactions.

When You Marry
new and revised
covering the gamut of personal relationships —from first date to last baby
by Evelyn M. Duvall and Reuben Hill

From Margaret Mead's **INTRODUCTION TO WOMEN:** ***The Variety and Meaning of Their Sexual Experience*** (New York: Dell Publishing Co., 1953) ❊ Since World War II, a new kind of marriage has developed in America, a marriage with greater frankness, greater articulateness, greater sharing, than any we have known before in this country—an early marriage, focused on having children in comradeship . . . It seems at present that the most serious challenge to our mid-twentieth-century style of marriage, with all its gaiety, its gallantry, its comradeliness, lies in this last third of life [from 50 to 75].

WHEN YOU MARRY by Evelyn Millis Duvall, Ph.D., and Reuben Hill, Ph.D. (New York: D.C. Heath & Co., 1953; revised edition) ❊ Sexual adjustment in marriage depends much more upon psychological than upon physical factors. Marriages are therefore more likely to be satisfying in this realm where the first sex information has been received from parents rather than acquired on the street . . .

Marriage is without doubt our favorite institution. Nine out of ten Americans marry at least once during their lifetime. Failure to marry can be attributed to personal factors having to do with unhappy childhood experiences, mother and father dependence, ineligibility because of American standards of beauty and glamor, and perfectionism in mate choices.

MARRIAGE MANNERS: ***A Set of Etiquette Pointers to Help Keep Magic in Your Marriage*** by Marjorie Binford Woods and Helen Flynn (New York: Bobbs-Merrill, 1955) ❊ It's the inconsistencies of actions and thoughts in women that baffle men. So try to uncomplicate yourself and think and say only only what you really mean . . . Cultivate a set of good bathroom manners right in the beginning. No fair "hogging" the bath, or spreading your belongings all over the place. Respect each other's privacy. Make it a closed-door policy. Start by being wifely right off, by running his bath for him and placing the bath mat and towels in their correct spots.

You'll merit the new title of "wife" from your honeymoon days on:

>> *if* — you refrain from kissing or cuddling up to him in front of people (or otherwise embarrassing him in public).

>> *if* — when you differ with each other you do so humorously and courteously.

>> *if* — you cultivate little secret signs and phrases, familiar only to the two of you, and keep them working.

>> *if* — you try never to burst into tears over imaginary hurt feelings and make him impatient with you over your lack of emotional control.

From the Introduction by Paul Popenoe, President, The American Institute of Family Relations, to CAN THIS MARRIAGE BE SAVED? by Paul Popenoe, Sc.D., and Dorothy Cameron Disney (New York: Macmillan, 1960) ❈ Today the American Institute of Family Relations [located in Los Angeles] has sixty-one counselors and associate counselors. During thirty years of operation, we have given intensive training to more than 300 marriage counselors. We have given shorter courses of training in colleges, universities and elsewhere over the country to more than 1500 other persons . . . During the last quarter of a century we have worked steadily to raise the standards of marriage counseling. Many people who claim to be marriage counselors are well meaning but untrained; others have scholastic training but in fields unrelated to counseling.

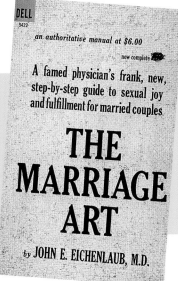

THE MARRIAGE ART by John E. Eichenlaub, M.D. (New York: Dell, 1962) ❈ At this point, each of you might find it worthwhile to assemble notes on your partner's responses. Then read Chapter One through Six and Chapter Twelve for further ideas to add to your notebook. Don't hesitate to discuss entries with your partner occasionally, perhaps even with demonstrations.

HOW TO MARRY SOMEONE YOU CAN LIVE WITH FOR LIFE by Dr. Leland E. Glover (Englewood Cliffs, NJ: Prentice-Hall, 1964): Recommended Educational Films ❈

Are You Ready for Marriage? (A marriage counselor discusses marital readiness and presents criteria.) Coronet Films.

Marriage Is a Partnership. (Helps couples learn about the problems they are likely to meet in marriage, and suggests that partners work together.) Coronet Films.

When Should I Marry? (A teen-age couple who want to get married talk with their minister about the problems of early marriage.) Distributed by the Text-Film Dept. of McGraw-Hill Book Co.

Worth Waiting For. (A young couple who desire sexual and emotional fulfillment during engagement decide that all the privileges of marriage are worth waiting for.) Distributed by Brigham Young University, Audio-Visual Communications.

SEX AND THE ADULT WOMAN by Birchall & Gerson (1965) ❋ Your husband must treat you with respect [and] be gentle and considerate, of course. But—at the same time—he must take you. Not only is this what you—as a woman—want more than anything else, it is also what he wants. Being taken in no way makes you less than your husband's equal. Just keep in mind that your fundamental biological urges and his are different . . . Wives who insist on "equality" in bed don't understand the true meaning of equality, and, frankly, desire less . . . Only if a woman respects her husband can she be happy in married life. She will not and cannot respect him unless he demonstrates his ultimate masculinity by taking her. Couples who fail to understand this basic truth are only half-married. Some are too "sophisticated," others are too "inhibited."

LETTERS TO KAREN: *On Keeping Love in Marriage* by Charlie W. Shedd (1965) ❋ There is one more thing to remember about wise wives and husbands whose sex drive seems unquenchable. The smart girls do not ration their men. They do not prescribe time, nor place, nor frequency, nor circumstances, nor manner . . . I have known dozens of men who left home for sexual entertainment and many of them belonged to women who insisted on always dictating the terms!

There is one other death knell to sexual happiness which you should guard carefully. This is sounded whenever a woman thinks of sex as a prize to be awarded when he has been an especially good boy. Whenever she holds it out to him as a bribe, she contributes a number one prospect for the women who go for casual affairs.

THE AFFAIR: *A Portrait of Extra-Marital Love in Contemporary America* by Morton Hunt (Cleveland, OH: NAL/World Publishing, 1969) ❋

>> Between one tenth and one quarter of first affairs last only one day;

>> Only a little over a tenth last more than one day but less than a month;

>> Close to half last more than a month but less than a year;

>> About one quarter last two or more years, but only a few of these endure four years or more.

From the book jacket of **THE MARRIAGE GRID** by Jane Srygley Mouton and Robert R. Blake (New York: McGraw-Hill, 1971) ❋ In *The Marriage Grid*, Drs. Mouton and Blake, the founders of Scientific Methods, Inc., offer a sound and simple system for analyzing intimate relationships and the marriage style that is apt to result. Using a simple numerical range, you place yourself on The Grid, after deciding how you measure up in terms of Concern for your Mate and Concern for What Happens . . . Check yourself out. If you are not satisfied with your relationship, perhaps you can find fresh possibilities by reading this book.

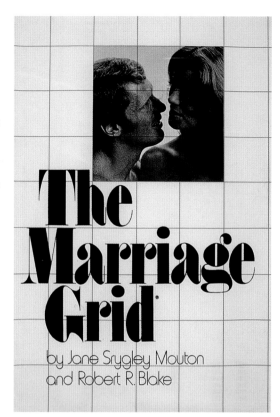

THE FUTURE OF MARRIAGE ("The Breakthrough Book That Introduced 'His and Hers' Marriages") by Jessie Bernard (New York: Bantam, 1972) ✳ *Swinging:* In their lifestyle, swingers are indistinguishable from their fellow suburbanites. It is only in their sexual activities that they are radical. Even so, they are not all that avant-garde in their marriages. In one sense, in fact, swinging is the simplest and least revolutionary modification of marriage as it is now structured that achieves both security and at least sexual excitement. It violates none of the marital vows: the partners remain committed to each other, they do not forsake each other, they continue—so they say—to love and cherish each other. All they do is share each other with other sexual partners.

From the contents of the April 28, 1972, issue of LIFE magazine, devoted to *"The Marriage Experiments: New Forms in a Cherished Institution"* ✳

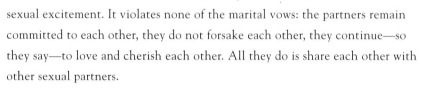

>> LIVING BY CONTRACT — "New Yorkers Martin and Aliz Shulman negotiated a written agreement splitting up family duties 50-50."

>> A MARRIAGE IN TROUBLE — "Near divorce, the Maxwells consult with a counselor between battles over liberation, sex, and the status quo."

>> UNMARRIED PARENTS — "Marjorie McCann and David Estridge have a new baby girl—but no license."

>> COLLECTIVE MARRIAGE — "Seven adults and four children keep house harmoniously together in Berkeley."

>> A LIFE QUESTIONAIRE — "What's happening to marriage?"

OPEN MARRIAGE: *A New Life Style for Couples* by Nena O'Neill and George O'Neill (New York: M. Evans & Co., 1972; Avon Books, 1973) ✳ Open marriage means an honest and open relationship between two people, based on the equal freedom and identity of both partners. It involves a verbal,

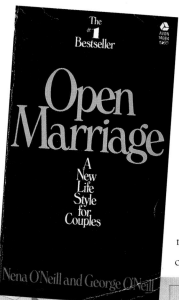

intellectual and emotional commitment to the right of each individual to grow within the marriage.

Open marriage is a non-manipulative relationship between man and woman. Neither is the object of total validation for the other's inadequacies or frustrations. Open marriage is a relationship of peers in which there is no need for dominance or submission, for comandeered restrictions, or stifling possessiveness. Each has the opportunity for growth and new experiences outside the marriage.

In a closed marriage, the couple does not exist in a one-plus-one relationship. Their ideal is to become fused into a single entity — a couple . . . The open marriage, in contrast, encourages growth for both husband and wife.

There is no doubt that innumerable contemporary couples are looking for some way out of the trap of their closed marriages . . . Our cultural attitudes toward the closed marriage are revealed in the colorful metaphors used to allude to the customary marriage: "she hooked him," "they got hitched," "you won't get me in that straightjacket," and "the ball and chain."

What we propose in open marriage is a complete revision from within the marriage—a revision that depends upon the two people involved . . . Marriage must be based upon a new openness. Only by writing their own open contract can couples achieve the flexibility they need to grow . . . Open marriage is expanded monogamy.

THE EROTIC LIFE OF THE AMERICAN WIFE by Natalie Gittelson (New York: Delacorte, 1972) ❋ If I had to describe in one word the general mood and tenor of the relationship between husband and wife in this country at this moment, I would choose, unhappily and unoriginally, alienation. Like the races and the generations, the sexes have probably never been less in accord than they are today . . . Among many American wives and husbands I met, sexual apathy ran high and sexual hostility higher. Wherever I went, evidence mounted that the act of copulation within middle-class marriage has descended too often to the status of trivial collusion.

THE BROTHERS SYSTEM FOR LIBERATED LOVE AND MARRIAGE by Dr. Joyce Brothers (New York: Peter H. Wydens, Inc., 1972) ❊ Marriage is not fulfilling the needs of women today. Women's needs have changed. Our society has changed. But marriage is still stuck back in the nineteenth century. I am convinced, nevertheless, that marriage is here to stay, and I mean the original husband-wife "'til death do us part" marriage. And I am equally convinced that it need not drive women crazy. Marriage can be liberated to meet the needs of contemporary women.

The majority of the books by the sex-oriented "marriage doctors" have a strong tinge of adolescent-boy fantasy. And no wonder: Most of the authors are men. And while many of them are men whose accomplishments I admire (some of them have been my mentors), I suspect that most of them have forgotten that marriage consists of a husband and a wife, two individuals who want to live together in happiness. They take a man's view of marriage. Very little attention is paid to the needs and desires of the wife . . . Too many marriage manuals leave women with the feeling that they are inadequate, second-class partners because they don't measure up to male standards. Most unhappy women are suffering from nothing but the masculine concept of the ideal marriage . . .

As for the writers and thinkers who advocate serial marriage, all I can say is, "Grow up." . . . Entering into a marriage is a more serious commitment than signing a contract to buy a new car.

From *"Why a New Marriage Manual?"* in **DR. RUTH'S GUIDE FOR MARRIED LOVERS** (New York: Warner Books, 1986) ❊ So there is a need for new marriage manuals written with post-Kinsey, post-Masters and Johnson, post-sexual revolution insight and information, and written for the present generation of the marrying kind of people. Those newly married, those marrying for the first time and those looking ardently for lasting closeness in second, third or tenth marriages . . .

Perhaps there are couples who care for their marriages easily. But you and your mate may not be like that, and you don't have to be. Yours may be a marriage with unavoidable struggle, a marriage of strong, somewhat opposing wills, and still be a splendid marriage! . . . Trust, communicate, share, work at your marriage, think about it, ask for help if you need help. Be realistic and always loving. Talk about your feelings but don't make them a burden. Stay together, realize that you're in this together. I have faith in you.

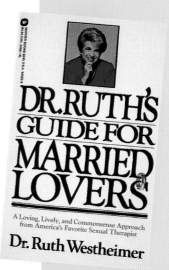

Our Choice for the Marriage Master of the New Millennium

John M. Gottman, a professor of psychology at the University of Washington in Seattle, is the founder of the Seattle Marital and Family Institute. Gottman affectionately refers to the Institute as "the marriage lab," and since the early 1970s he has been conducting experiments there intended to shed light on that greatest of all modern mysteries: how marriages work, and what has derailed them when they don't. Dr. Gottman is the author of such tomes as *Marriage Clinic: A Scientifically Based Marital Therapy* (Norton, 1999), *Seven Principles for Making Marriage Work* (Crown, 1999) and *Why Marriages Succeed or Fail: And How You Can Make Yours Last* (Simon & Schuster, 1997), all based on the work he performs in "the lab."

Gottman's particular brand of marriage counseling involves hooking up husband and wife to a bank of sensors that can measure their heart rates, blood flow, respiration, and perspiration as he and she each discuss their perceptions of the marriage. After two days of such testing, observing body language, facial expressions, and other subliminal signposts, Gottman—who is on his second marriage—has a fix on where the couple's problems lie. "With a couple of minutes of videotape, we can predict with ninety percent accuracy what's going to happen to a marriage," Gottman told a reporter who profiled him for *The Chronicle of Higher Education.* Then, after analyzing what he has seen and measured, Gottman and his team go to work—if the subjects are willing. "What we do is formalize the process of repair." (In April 1999, Gottman and his marriage lab were also profiled in a flattering manner by *Newsweek.*)

Professor Gottman, the editors of *Wedding Bell Blues* salute you as the man most needed by the married in the new millennium. Now, let's go to the videotape!

Whom the Gods Would Betroth

Part 1

THE MOST EPOCHAL MARRIAGES OF THE 20TH CENTURY

The pop-culture seismographs registered record-setting tremors when these unions were announced:

♥♥ The standard by which all others are measured: Edward and "Wally" Simpson, The Duke & Duchess of Windsor. In 1936, Edward VIII renounced the throne of England for the love of American socialite (and divorcee) Wallis Warfield Simpson—a *beau geste* very few of us will ever have the chance to make, even if we had the nerve to do it. (Which, face it, not a one of us would.) And if you don't agree that their 1937 wedding was the grandest of the century, please explain why, in 1998, a collector paid $26,000 at auction for a slice of their wedding cake.

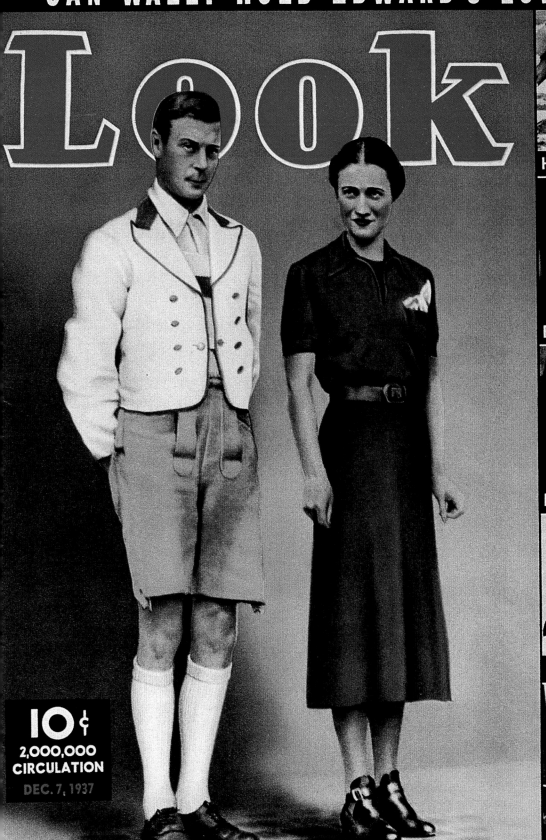

CAN WALLY HOLD EDWARD'S LOVE?

Look

10¢
2,000,000
CIRCULATION
DEC. 7, 1937

HEROES

BRIDES

BRAVE BEAUTY

SNOW WHITE

CANTOR

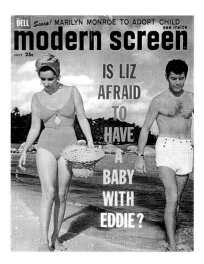

♥♥ Grace Kelly and the Prince of Monaco, 1956. About which, more anon.

♥♥ Bogie and Bacall, 1945. A May-September marriage? So what? All the world loves a happy lover—twice so if he's married to another happy lover. Don't you want to see Bogie smile?

♥♥ Liz Taylor and Eddie Fisher, 1959; Liz Taylor and Richard Burton, 1964 (tie). About which, much, much more anon.

♥♥ Clark Gable and Carole Lombard, 1939. They'd been "seeing" each other since 1932, when they costarred in their only film together, *No Man of Her Own*.

♥♥ Marilyn Monroe and "Joltin'" Joe DiMaggio: The queen of Hollywood joined kingdoms with the emperor of American sports for a rocky ten months in 1954. Then, in 1956, the queen of Hollywood relinquished her kingdom to unite with one of America's leading Jewish intellectuals, playwright Arthur Miller. That marriage lasted longer, but seemed just as rocky as the one that preceded it.

♥♥ Frank Sinatra and Ava Gardner, 1951; Sinatra and Mia Farrow, 1966 (tie). Both marriages created headlines by the truckload, from ecstatic beginnings to bitter, bitter endings.

♥♥ Rita Hayworth and Orson Welles, 1943; Rita and Prince Aly Khan, 1949 (tie). From the crown prince of Hollywood to the prince of Morocco, the lovely Rita seemed to have it all. Too bad both husbands proved to be utter jerks.

♥♥ Douglas Fairbanks and Mary Pickford, 1921. At the time, they reigned as the undisputed king and queen of Hollywood—they were two of the four founders of the revolutionary United Artists studio—so their marriage took on the import of the unification of France and England.

♥♥ Lady Diana Spencer and Prince Charles, July 21, 1981. Not because of what their marriage meant to the Brits, but because of what it meant to us, here, on the other side of the Atlantic.

Part 2

A CENTURY OF HOLLYWOOD HONEYMOONS, MARRIAGES, AND DIVORCES—PLUS A FEW REALLY TAWDRY AFFAIRS

♥♥ The first wedding of Hollywood royalty, between silent film superstars Douglas Fairbanks and "America's Sweetheart" Mary Pickford, took place in 1921. In a 1927 article in *Photoplay* magazine, "The Married Life of Doug and Mary," Adela Rogers St. John anointed them as having "the most successful famous marriage the world has ever known . . . It comes as near to being perfect as any human relationship I have ever encountered in this imperfect universe. To go into their home and see them together is one of those things that gives you back your lost dreams." The perfect couple made just one picture together, the reportedly wretched *The Taming of the Shrew* in 1929 (spouses Liz Taylor and Richard Burton would make their own version in 1967), and were divorced in 1936.

♥♥ Joan Crawford and Douglas Fairbanks, Jr., wed in 1929 and separated in 1932, after numerous charges of affairs on both sides eroded the relationship. A final divorce decree was handed down in 1934. She next married actor Franchot Tone on October 11, 1935; they were divorced in 1940.

♥♥ George Burns and Gracie Allen, married since 1926, spent their lives performing together on the vaudeville stage, in Hollywood, on radio, and on television. She died in 1964; he went on with his solo routine well into his nineties.

♥♥ Barbara Stanwyck and Robert Taylor, two of Hollywood's most glamorous movie actors, wed in 1939 and remained married until 1951—one of the longer marriages between two major screen stars. Previously, rising star Stanwyck had been married to one-time vaudeville headliner Frank Fay, whose talents didn't translate when he moved to Hollywood. Their ill-fated marriage, with her rising to stardom and him descending into obscurity, often has been pointed to as the basis for the plots of *What Price Hollywood?* (1932) and *A Star Is Born* (1937, 1954, 1976).

♥♥ After a seven-year affair, Clark Gable, the King of Hollywood, eloped with irrepressible actress Carole Lombard in March 1939, three weeks after he was finally granted a divorce by wife Ria. The happy couple flew to Kingman, Arizona, to get married, where a minister and Lombard's former high school principal graced the ceremony. But Lombard died in a plane crash during a war bond drive in the winter of '42, sending both the King and all of Hollywood into mourning. Their romance was not-quite immortalized in the crummy 1976 film *Gable and Lombard,* starring the game but overmatched James Brolin and Jill Clayburgh.

♥♥ Lucille Ball wed Cuban-born band leader Desi Arnaz on November 30, 1940. They divorced twenty years later, but managed to leave behind as a monument to their union a media empire of unparalleled scope. The centerpiece of that empire, of course, was their classic weekly television show, *I Love Lucy,* arguably the most popular sitcom of all time. Lucy had originally starred in *My Favorite Husband,* a radio version of the show, in 1949 opposite Richard Denning. But when CBS decided to develop the concept into a TV series, she insisted that Desi—a womanizer and drinker of Olympian stature—replace Denning as her small-screen spouse, thus keeping him front and center ten hours a day, five days a week, thirty-nine weeks of the year. By all accounts, the professional pairing did help on the homefront—for a while.

♥♥ Mickey Rooney married Georgia peach (and MGM contract player) Ava Gardner in January of 1942. Just prior to the ceremony, Rooney took her to meet his mother so they could tell her the news together. "I guess he ain't been into your pants yet" was her dry evaluation of their announcement, Gardner recalled in her memoir *Ava: My Story*. MGM publicist Les Petersen traveled with them on their honeymoon in Monterey, at the behest of studio head Louis B. Mayer. A year later Mickey and Ava separated; they divorced on May 21, 1943.

♥♥ Dick Powell and Joan Blondell, married in 1936, separated in 1941, one year after the release of their film *I Want a Divorce*. Their divorce was finalized in 1945, and on August 19 of that year, Powell married young screen star June Allyson. Blondell waited until 1947 to remarry; her choice was Mike Todd, who in 1957 would become Elizabeth Taylor's third husband.

♥♥ In 1945, erstwhile number-one box-office star Shirley Temple found herself as just another cute seventeen-year-old searching for a hit movie. Then she married handsome John Agar on September 19, at Hollywood's Wilshire Methodist Church, and was once again America's Sweetheart. Shirley's classmates from the Westlake School served as her bridesmaids, but the wedding was held up half an hour until mogul David Selznick arrived. Shirley's marriage to Agar was the delight of the Hollywood fan magazines, who covered the birth of their daughter, Linda Susan, and their costarring roles in John Ford's *Ft. Apache* as if those events were on the scale of the Yalta summit. Alas, in 1949, just months after *Modern Screen* magazine published their special issue about Shirley and her ideal home life, she and Agar divorced.

♥♥ Eleven days after divorcing third wife Mayo Methot on May 10, 1945, Humphrey Bogart married twenty-year-old Lauren Bacall at the Ohio farm of author Louis Bromfield. The newlyweds then repaired straightaway to the Warner Brothers lot, postponing their honeymoon for a more convenient time. They remained happily married until Bogie's hideous death from cancer in January 14, 1957.

♥♥ Orson Welles wed Rita Hayworth on September 7, 1943, in Santa Monica, on her day off from filming *Cover Girl*. But no sooner had he won her (from such serious suitors as Victor Mature) than he lost interest, even as she prepared to bear their child. By 1946, they were estranged. While a brief reconciliation followed later that year as they prepared to film *The Lady from Shanghai*, by the time the film was actually released, in May 1948, Rita and Orson were divorced.

Then, in May 1949, Rita wed Prince Aly Khan in the small French town of Vallauris, despite a tardy if energetic effort by Welles to win her back. There was both a civil and, the following night, a more private Moslem ceremony, held at the Chateau de l'Horizon. Khan's wedding presents to her included a 12-carat diamond ring, cash, jewels, four racehorses, and a $12,000 Alpha Romeo. During the two-plus years they were married, Rita stayed far away from Hollywood, as befit the Princess Khan. But after they separated in 1951, she returned to filmmaking with a vengeance. Her first post-Aly movie, *Affair in Trinidad*, was advertised by Columbia in 1952 with the joyful slogan, "Rita Is Back!"

♥♥ MGM star Judy Garland married MGM star director Vincente Minnelli on June 13, 1945, at her mother's house in Los Angeles, one week after her divorce from bandleader David Rose was finalized. Vincente was thirty-one, Judy just twenty-four. Ira Gershwin served as best man. Four years later, the marriage was over, leaving little Liza in its wake.

♥♥ Married since 1940, Jane Wyman and Ronald Reagan were granted a divorce in 1948. Four years later, Ronnie married Nancy Davis, and the rest, as they say, is history. Footnote: His only film with Nancy was the 1957 war pic *Hellcats of the Navy*.

♥♥ Roy Rogers wed costar Dale Evans on New Year's Eve of 1948 at a ranch in Oklahoma, a year after the death of his first wife. Dale had also been widowed, at the tender age of seventeen—but once she and Roy got hitched, it would be happy trails from that point on.

♥♥ Ingrid Bergman and Dr. Peter Lindstrom were granted a divorce by proxy in Mexico on February 10, 1949, after her affair with Italian film director Roberto Rossellini shocked the nation. (Our nation, anyway.) The same Mexican judge married Bergman and Rossellini by proxy a few minutes later. Their first film together, *Stromboli*, was denounced (on principal; no one had yet seen it) by America's amateur legions of decency. Its 1950 release in the U.S. was covered by *LIFE* magazine, amid boycotts by theater owners and the yawns of the few moviegoers who bothered to see it.

♥♥ Elizabeth Taylor got married for the first—but hardly the last—time on May 6, 1950, at age eighteen. The lucky groom was Nicky Hilton, heir to the Hilton Hotel fortune. At age nineteen, that union already dissolved, Liz selected British actor Michael Wilding, who was twice her age, to be her second husband. Her third husband, millionaire impresario and sportsman Mike Todd, whom she married in 1957, had a son from an earlier marriage who was older than Liz.

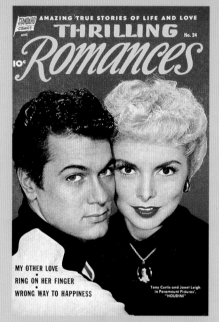

♥♥ Ava Gardner married Frank Sinatra on November 7, 1951, just weeks after his divorce from first wife Nancy was finalized. They separated in October 1953, and divorce proceedings commenced in 1954. "Perhaps I expected too much from my husbands, and they inevitably disappointed me," Ava later mused in her autobiography, *Ava: My Story*. Along with Rooney and Sinatra, she was once also married to bandleader Artie Shaw. "I tried damn hard with all three," Ava ruefully recalled. "One of the strangest things about my trio of failed marriages was that the marriage bond seemed to be a shackle that manacled us together. Once divorced, we enjoyed each other and retained a deep friendship. And more than anyone else, that was true between Frank and me."

♥♥ Bronx-born heartthrob Bernard Schwartz, known to moviegoers as Tony Curtis, married blonde bombshell Janet Leigh (nee Jeanette Morrison) in 1951. For a time, they reigned as America's sweethearts, starring together in such films as *Houdini* (1953) and *The Black Shield of Falworth* (1954), but by 1962, their union had sundered.

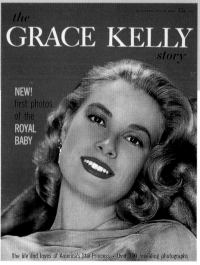

♥♥ Grace Kelly wed Prince Rainier III of Monaco twice in 1956: first on April 18 (civil ceremony), then on April 19 (Catholic ceremony). The press immediately dubbed it the Wedding of the Century, supplanting the most recent candidate, the 1949 nuptials of Prince Aly Khan and Rita Hayworth. "I don't want this wedding to become a circus," a cranky Prince Rainier (who also carried 141 other formal titles, including His Serene Highness) huffed by way of explanation when he banned most of the 150 photographers from covering the ceremony. Grace (who was given 140 titles upon marrying Rainier) managed to exclude gossip doyens Hedda Hopper, Louella Parsons, and Sheila Graham from being invited to the affair. Three thousand citizens of Monaco attended the reception for the civil ceremony; 600 star-studded guests came the next day to the Cathedral of St. Nicholas and, after vows were again exchanged, watched Rainier cut the six-foot-high cake with his sword. Later that afternoon, the entire wedding party sallied forth to watch a soccer game at National Stadium.

♥♥ They had to resolve conflicts between their different religious back-grounds, delaying their nuptials, which millions of American fans had been breathlessly awaiting. But the marriage of twenty-four-year-old screen star Debbie Reynolds and twenty-six-year-old Eddie Fisher, the "crooning wonder of the decade" (as *Motion Picture* magazine anointed him) finally took place on September 26, 1955—though not with a rabbi and a Protestant minister presiding, as they'd originally planned. They were quickly dubbed America's Sweethearts by that bible of fandom, *Photoplay* magazine, which then celebrated this historic union in its December issue with the piece "A Dream Come True." Fisher was considered quite a catch: he had 1500 fan clubs spread around the country, and reported earnings of $750,000 for 1954.

All would be well until Mike Todd, a pal of Eddie's and the third husband of Elizabeth Taylor, was killed in a plane crash in March 1958, leaving Eddie to console the fabulously gorgeous widow. After several intimate consolation sessions, Eddie Fisher and Elizabeth Taylor were married at Temple Beth Sholom (Liz converted to Judaism) in Las Vegas on May 12, 1959—the very day his divorce decree from Debbie was finalized. Cries of "homewrecker!" were heard across the land.

But the fun was just beginning. After working together in the film *Butterfield 8*, in which Eddie had a small role, they traveled to England in September 1960 so Liz could begin filming her signature role as the eponymous *Cleopatra*. It was a job for which Twentieth Century Fox was paying her a cool million, making her the first actor ever to command such a sum. Her costar was the magnetic (if famously conceited) British actor Richard Burton, whose most recent gig was performing as the lead in the Broadway production of *Camelot*. According to the article "When Liz Met Dick" in the April 1998 *Vanity Fair*, Eddie was being paid $150,000 by Fox to babysit his diva wife. And Liz would need his TLC, as she was stricken with double pneumonia shortly after filming commenced (this was, after all, London in the winter). She fell into a coma and needed an emergency tracheotomy on March 4, 1961, a near-death experience that many attributed to her winning the Best Actress Academy Award for *Butterfield 8* later that month.

With the production now moving to the more clement Rome, Liz regained her health and returned to work opposite Burton (who played Mark Antony; Rex Harrison was Caesar), with whom she now began the affair that rocked the world. (It was officially announced for all to ponder in Louella Parson's syndicated gossip column of March 10, 1962.) But Eddie Fisher and Sybil Burton, the about-to-be-deserted spouses, didn't go down without a fight. After many tearful spats among and between lovers and spouses, oceans of tabloid ink, assorted separations, and a whole lot of enthusiastic shagging, the affair culminated with Liz being granted an uncontested Mexican divorce from Eddie on March 5, 1964. (By now, *Cleopatra* had been released and found wanting by both American critics and audiences). Ten days later, in Montreal, Liz and Dick were wed (her ring: the 69.42-carat Cartier-Burton diamond) by a Unitarian minister. The very next day the Burtons travelled to Toronto, where he rejoined the production of *Hamlet* in which he had been starring.

During the nine years of their marriage, they played spouses in *The V.I.P.s*, *Who's Afraid of Virginia Woolf?* (a second Oscar for Liz), *The Taming of the Shrew*, and a little-seen made-for-TV film, *Divorce: His / Divorce: Hers*, which was broadcast in 1973, the same year she divorced Burton. She remarried him in 1975, then re-divorced him a few months later.

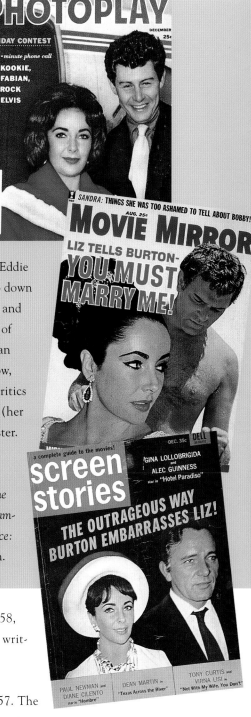

♥♥ Paul Newman and Joanne Woodward married in January 1958, after he was granted a divorce by his first wife, Jacqueline. At this writing, more than forty years later, they remain happily married.

♥♥ Natalie Wood and Robert Wagner eloped and married in 1957. The occasion was immortalized in the April 1958 issue of *Photoplay* magazine, which published a photo spread entitled "Natalie and Bob: Our Wedding." The handsome couple divorced in 1963—in large part because of Natalie's steamy affair with Warren Beatty, her costar in *Splendor in the Grass*—but they remarried in 1972, to Hollywood's joy. They remained together until Natalie tragically drowned while sailing off the Catalina coast in November 1981.

♥♥ Barbra Streisand and Elliot Gould met while appearing in the Broadway show *I Can Get It for You Wholesale* in 1962. They got married by a justice of the peace in Carson City, Nevada, on September 21, 1963, while Barbra was appearing for the first time as a Vegas headliner. Shortly thereafter, she began rehearsals for the role that would make her a star, as Fanny Brice in the Broadway smash *Funny Girl*. "Sometimes I think Barbra is twenty-two going on eight," her new husband remarked of her. Their marriage began foundering almost immediately, although they staggered on into the Seventies before calling it quits.

♥♥ Flower child Mia Farrow might not have seemed an especially logical match for living legend Frank Sinatra, as he was more than twice her age and was still (if just barely) in the heyday of his Rat Pack "Chairman of the Board" persona. But, as Mia described in her 1997 autobiography *What Falls Away*, "Difficult years had shaped us both. Our needs were enormous and not simple. We understood ourselves and each other so little, and whatever comprehension we may have had, we could not convey. Blindly we sought completion in each other." They were secretly married in Las Vegas on June 19, 1966, sans families, in a four-minute ceremony, and honeymooned in London while Frank filmed *The Naked Runner*. But when she decided to play the lead in Roman Polanski's *Rosemary's Baby* instead of taking the role Frank had offered her in his own flick, *The Detective*, the marriage was finished. In August 1968 they got a Mexican divorce in Juarez.

♥♥ Elvis Presley, though he was no longer the world's most popular singer, was still an international star when, on May 1, 1967, he married long-time flame Priscilla Beaulieu in Las Vegas; it was a small, ten-minute ceremony at the Aladdin Hotel. He was thirty-two, she was twenty-one. They honeymooned in Palm Springs and had a big ol' reception back at Graceland upon their return.

Elvis had met Priscilla while he was stationed in Germany in 1959, where he courted her with extreme caution—as befit a man in his twenties dating a fourteen-year-old. Somehow he convinced her dad, a captain in the U.S. Army, to let her complete her education back in Memphis, where she attended Immaculate Conception High School, followed by a stint at the Patricia Stevens Finishing School. After six rocky years, they were divorced on October 11, 1973, with Elvis well into his Vegas reincarnation phase. A few years later, bloated and pathetic, he was found dead in his bathroom of a drug overdose. Priscilla went on to costar in films like *Naked Gun* and had the dubious pleasure of watching their daughter, Lisa Marie, marry the oh-so-peculiar superstar Michael Jackson, a marriage that seemed to last about twenty minutes.

♥♥ Michelle Phillips, the achingly beautiful golden girl of the California band The Mamas and the Papas, married actor/director/lunatic Dennis Hopper in 1971. The marriage lasted one week; as a parting shot, Michelle suggested that he commit suicide.

♥♥ Steve McQueen stole Ali McGraw away from her husband, Paramount mogul Robert Evans, while the two were filming *The Getaway* in 1971. They got married in 1973 and remained hitched until 1978. He died in 1980 of a heart attack at age fifty.

STEVE McQUEEN/ALI MacGRAW IN "THE GETAWAY" A FIRST ARTISTS PRESENTATION CO-STARRING **BEN JOHNSON** · **AL LETTIERI** AND **SALLY STRUTHERS** AS "FRAN" SCREENPLAY BY WALTER HILL · FROM THE NOVEL BY JIM THOMPSON · MUSIC BY QUINCY JONES · A SOLAR/FOSTER-BROWER PRODUCTION · PRODUCED BY DAVID FOSTER AND MITCHELL BROWER · DIRECTED BY SAM PECKINPAH FILMED IN TODD-AO 35 · TECHNICOLOR® **PG** PARENTAL GUIDANCE SUGGESTED A NATIONAL GENERAL PICTURES RELEASE

♥♥ Farrah Fawcett and Lee "The Six Million Dollar Man" Majors wed on July 28, 1973. They split up in 1979, after Farrah became an international superstar thanks to the TV series, *Charlie's Angels*.

♥♥ Famed hothead Sean Penn married pop icon Madonna in August 1985. They were finally divorced in 1989, after withdrawing an abortive divorce action in 1987. Ten years later, Sean still referred to Madonna as "my first wife," instead of by name.

♥♥ Kim Basinger and Alec Baldwin got married in 1993, after the lovely-dovey duo performed together in an unsuccessful 1991 film called, appropriately enough, *The Marrying Man*.

♥♥ Warren Beatty and Annette Benning were married on January 1992, after acting together in the 1991 film *Bugsy*. Since then, they have costarred in only one movie, a ponderous remake of the 1939 classic *Love Affair* (a.k.a. *An Affair to Remember*); released in 1994, it was a resounding flop.

♥♥ Former Glen Ridge, New Jersey, hunk Tom Cruise and Aussie beauty Nicole Kidman met while filming the bombastic *Days of Thunder* in 1990. They fell in love and got married the following year (after Tom ditched first wife Mimi Rogers, that is). Becoming one of Hollywood's premier power duos, they made a whole bunch of successful movies without each other, and one or two with, such as the forgettable *Far and Away* (1992). They earned a *Time* magazine cover heralding the release of their joint effort under the late Stanley Kubrick's direction, the reportedly ultra-erotic thriller *Eyes Wide Shut*, in which they play a married couple who delve into the seamy underworld of promiscuous sex.

♥♥ Gen-X stars Uma Thurman and Ethan Hawke wed on May Day of 1998.

♥♥ Superdiva Barbra Streisand and demi-star James Brolin were married in a very secret ceremony on July 1, 1998, at her Malibu estate.

♥♥ Hollywood heavyweights Demi Moore and Bruce Willis announced their separation on June 24, 1998. After nearly ten years of marriage, they had made only one film together, the instantly forgotten *Mortal Thoughts* in 1991, but they were Hollywood's most visible—and bankable—power couple of the Nineties. But then, "What is marriage?," Willis opined in a 1997 interview with *Playboy*. "No woman is going to satisfy a man's natural impulse to procreate, procreate, procreate." In a 1998 interview, Bruce also told *USA Today*, "I see us married one day at a time." Now it's time out.

Part 3
THEY NEVER MARRIED: HOLLYWOOD'S MOST "ALMOST" COUPLES

Admit it—you always thought you'd wake up one morning and, over your coffee, read about the secret but oh-so-fabulous nuptials of these high-profile, long-linked couples. And then one day, you realized: it never happened. And never would.

♥♥ Greta Garbo and John Gilbert.

♥♥ William Randolph Hearst and Marion Davies.

♥♥ Gloria Swanson and Joseph Kennedy, Sr.

♥♥ Jean Harlow and William Powell.

♥♥ Charlie Chaplin and Paulette Goddard (although he claimed they were secretly married at sea back around 1938).

♥♥ Spencer Tracy and Katharine Hepburn.

♥♥ Frank Sinatra and Lauren Bacall. (When she announced their engagement in 1958 before he was ready to make it public, Sinatra immediately—and permanently—dumped her. Whatta prince!)

♥♥ Warren Beatty and Julie Christie.

♥♥ Al Pacino and Jill Clayburgh.

♥♥ Woody Allen and Diane Keaton.

♥♥ Warren Beatty and Diane Keaton.

♥♥ Kurt Russell and Goldie Hawn.

♥♥ Jack Nicholson and Angelica Huston.

♥♥ Julia Roberts and Kiefer Sutherland.
(They came mighty close, though, in 1991, when scores of wedding guests awaited them on a sound-stage at the Fox Studios, where the ceremony was to be held. But Julia called it off just hours before the appointed time.)

♥♥ Woody Allen and Mia Farrow. (Eeeks!)

♥♥ Brad Pitt and Gwyneth Paltrow.

Part 4

THE GOSPEL TRUTH: HOLLYWOOD FAN MAGS GIVE US THE LOW-DOWN

Long before *People* magazine, let alone *Entertainment Weekly* or *Us*, the weekly magazine reading of millions of Americans included the category known as the Hollywood fan mag. In their heyday, from the 1920s through the 1960s, there were literally scores of these movie-oriented magazines proliferating on the newsstand, with titles like *Photoplay*, *Silver Screen*, *Movie Mirror*, *Motion Picture*, *Picture Play*, and *Screen Romances*. Each month these periodicals, with their lovingly rendered portraits of the top screen stars of the day, carried tens of thousands of words about those hundreds upon hundreds of actors and actresses who, for at least one brief, shining moment, had earned the right to be idolized.

Those movie stars were the analogs to the bright lights of the "real" world—the moguls, power brokers, heirs and heiresses whose activities dominated the pages of the mainstream magazines. The truth of the matter was quite simple: in those dark, pre-*People* days, the twain rarely met. A popular mainstream weekly such as *Look*, for instance, would have the mandate to present the glorious, world-shaking romance of the Duke and Duchess of Windsor as a cover story. In that world, not even Hollywood's own royal couple, Clark Gable and Carole Lombard, had a chance of getting equivalent coverage.

Case in point: "Can Wally Hold Edward's Love?" in *Look's* December 7, 1937 issue, which posed the most profound question of the day: "Can Wally hold the Duke in spite of Royal snubs?" After Edward VIII, the Duke of Windsor, abdicated his throne for the love of American socialite Wallace Simpson, the entire House of Windsor was thrown into a royal snit. *Look* was there to chronicle the outrageous slights and cold shoulders the brave couple received after their Paris honeymoon from such bluebloods as the Duke and Duchess of Kent. Why, their wedding party found no royal relatives in attendance—a slight with which even readers of America's ten-cent weeklies could commiserate. "My wife and I are neither content nor willing to lead a purely inactive life," the proud, unbowed Duke of Windsor told the press. Hear, hear!

However, since the 1920s, modern American royalty has been crowned in the zip code now familiar to all as 90210. That is why ninety percent of the covers of *People* are devoted to entertainment figures, even though inside one can find human interest stories drawn from the lives of the hoi polloi. (Quick—Who was on the cover of the first issue of *People* back in 1974? If you guessed Mia Farrow, give yourself a free year's subscription.)

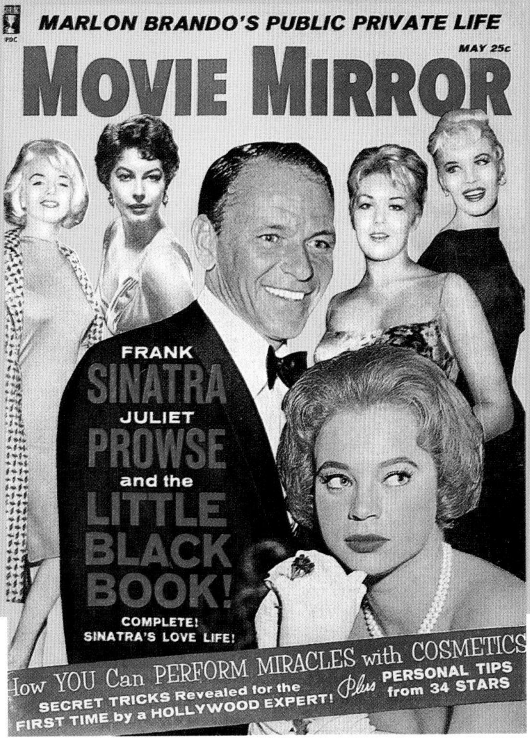

And so, straight from the Hollywood of yore, we now present you with a dozen of these once-urgent bulletins from the fan mags about marriages about to commence, and marriages about to dissolve—all of them now long over, none of them entirely forgotten:

1) "'Don't Elope,' Says Gene Tierney," by Helen Wallace [*Hollywood*, May 1942]: "Ever since her widely publicized runaway marriage to Count Oleg Cassini, Gene Tierney is deluged with letters from young people who seek her advice on their romantic problems. 'What I have told most of them,' she says, 'is this: that in spite of my own elopement, I personally don't favor elopements at all! Marriage is the greatest time in a girl's life and that's when her family should be with her.'"

(The gorgeous Tierney stayed married to Cassini until 1952.)

2) "Who Will Be Elizabeth Taylor's Next Husband?" by Aline Mosby [*Photoplay*, January 1957]: "Whether or not it's Mike Todd, chances are he'll be an older man . . . Lost between two worlds, Liz, the child, searches for a father, the woman for a lover."

(Liz did marry Todd on Groundhog's Day in 1957. But after his untimely death in a March 1958 plane crash, she would go on to wed a series of new husbands. None of them, though, would be a man as senior as Mike Todd.)

3) "Hollywood Goes Marriage Crazy" by Frank Elliot [*Motion Picture*, September 1939]: "In no year has there been such a stampede of stars into matrimony as 1939. What's behind this marriage epidemic?"

(We're just guessing, but how about the advent of the Second World War?)

4) "Husbands Are Wonderful!" by Virginia Wilson [*Modern Screen*, May 1946]: "'Husbands!' sighs Shirley Temple. 'They get hotel rooms, fix car doors, praise your cooking—and look so helpless when they're sick!'"

(Shirley divorced her wonderful husband, John Agar, in 1949.)

MOVIE MIRROR

MAY 25¢

FRANK SINATRA JULIET PROWSE and the LITTLE BLACK BOOK!

COMPLETE! SINATRA'S LOVE LIFE!

How YOU Can PERFORM MIRACLES with COSMETICS

SECRET TRICKS Revealed for the FIRST TIME by a HOLLYWOOD EXPERT! *Plus* PERSONAL TIPS from 34 STARS

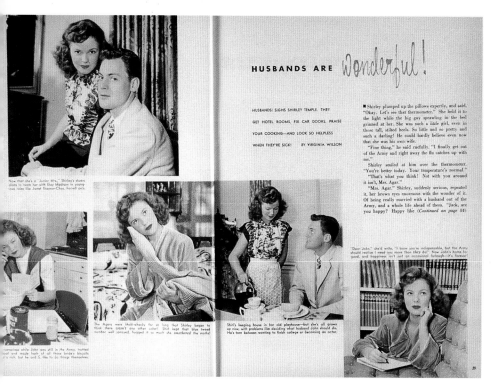

HUSBANDS ARE *Wonderful!*

HUSBANDS! SIGHS SHIRLEY TEMPLE. THEY

GET HOTEL ROOMS, FIX CAR DOORS, PRAISE

YOUR COOKING—AND LOOK SO HELPLESS

WHEN THEY'RE SICK! BY VIRGINIA WILSON

■ Shirley plumped up the pillows expertly, and said, "Okay. Let's see that thermometer." She held it to the light while the big guy sprawling in the bed grinned at her. She was such a *little* girl, even in those tall, stilted heels. So little and so pretty and such a darling! He could hardly believe even now that she was his own wife.

"Fine thing," he said ruefully. "I finally get out of the Army and right away the flu catches up with me."

Shirley smiled at him over the thermometer. "You're better today. Your temperature's normal."

"That's what you think! Not with you around it isn't, Mrs. Agar."

"Mrs. Agar," Shirley, suddenly serious, repeated it, her brown eyes enormous with the wonder of it. Of being really married with a husband out of the Army, and a whole life ahead of them. "Jack, are you happy? Happy like *(Continued on page 84)*

Captions within photo spread:

"Now that she's a 'Junior Mrs.,' Shirley's studio plans to team her with Guy Madison in young-love roles, like Janet Gaynor–Chas. Farrell pics.

The Agars were khaki-whacky for so long that Shirley began to think there wasn't any other color! Shirl kept that blue tweed number well sprayed, hugged it so much she smothered the moths!

Shirl's keeping house in her old playhouse—but she's all grown up now, with problems like deciding what husband John should do. He's torn between wanting to finish college or becoming an actor.

"Dear John," she'd write, "I know you're indispensable, but the Army should realize I need you more than they do!" Now John's home for good, and happiness isn't just an occasional furlough—it's forever!

—conscious while John was still in the Army, trotted out and made hash of all those bride's biscuits J.'s rich, but he and S. like to do things themselves.

(Continued on page 84)

5) "Dodging the Wedding Ring" by Ruth Biery [*Photoplay*, February 1928]: "Here are five reasons why [Hollywood actresses] do not leave home—for a husband: Because divorces are too prevalent in Hollywood. Because men, particularly when they are husbands, are jealous. Because studio hours prevent a real domestic life. Because they love their work. Because they want to be loved for themselves alone, and not because they are rich and famous. So they say."

(Makes sense to us. But then, where do all Hollywood divorces come from?)

6) "Hollywood's Unmarried Husbands and Wives," by Kirtley Baskette [*Photoplay*, January 1934]: "'Just friends' to the world at large—yet nowhere has domesticity taken on so unique a character as in this unconventional fold."

(The writer goes on to cite such couples as Clark Gable and Carole Lombard [who would later wed], Barbara Stanwyck and Robert Taylor [who would get married the following year], George Raft and Virginia Pine [like Gable, he was not yet free from his wife of record], and Charlie Chaplin and Paulette Goddard [who, some later claimed, were married at sea in a ceremony that may have been less than legal and binding].)

7) "Sonny & Cher: The Brutal Truth Behind the Divorce!" [*Modern Screen*, June 1974]: "After all, what is *Sonny and Cher* without Sonny *and* Cher? [But] they just couldn't get along . . . There were even whispers that he had thrown her out of a window, but they were totally ridiculous and without a bit of truth. But that was what we heard."

(Do you *believe* there's life after love?)

8) "The Future They Face" [Debbie Reynolds & Eddie Fisher] by Norma Keller [*Motion Picture*, May 1955]: "A mixed marriage—and a great love! Can Debbie and Eddie reconcile the two?"

(Of course, they did manage to reconcile the two—at least, until Liz Taylor butted in. Incidentally, this piece was illustrated by a painting of Debbie in a formal gown executed by Charles Binger, "a member of the Royal Society of Portrait Artists," thoughtfully commissioned by the editors of *Motion Picture* for all the fans who wouldn't be invited to their idols' wedding.)

9) "I Saw Rita Hayworth Marry Aly Khan," by Louella O. Parsons [*Photoplay*, August 1949]: "Whether she will be happy I am not certain. Can any American girl, much less one as spoiled as Rita has been, adjust to any such existence as she has set for herself? This I know—it isn't going to be easy."

(It wasn't; Rita divorced Aly less than two years later.)

10) "The Awful Truth" by Sonia Lee [*Movieland*, November 1944]: "What's behind the Grant-Hutton break-up? Unfortunately, 'the truth' is that their marriage had too many counts against it, at the start. It just couldn't last."

(The title of this article bears the same title as Cary Grant's famous romantic comedy from 1937, discussed elsewhere in this volume. And the awful truth is, none of his five marriages did last very long.)

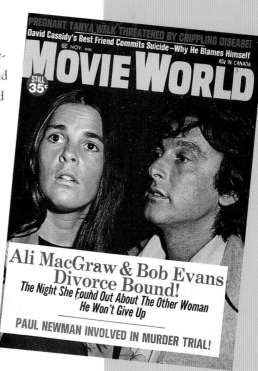

11) " 'I'll Never Marry Again, and Yet—' " by Sonia Lee [*Hollywood*, September 1939]: "Joan Crawford turns her brilliant mind to analysis of the condition that has wrecked two marriages and that almost ruined her acting career twice."

(The lusty Joan would marry again, and yet again— and how!)

12) "Ali and Bob Are Headed for Divorce!" by Eve Steele [*Movie World*, November 1971]: " 'It's very simple, really,' says one studio source. 'Bob wants Ali to work—she wants to be a housewife. Bob wants another woman—Ali the actress!' "

(Paramount studio head Robert Evans would end up with neither Ali McGraw—the freespirited actress ran off with actor Steve McQueen during the filming of the Peckinpah film, *The Getaway*.)

Eight Exquisite Comic Books Devoted to the Agonies of Marriage

True Bride-to-Be Romances (1956-58)

True Bride's Experiences (1956-58)

Bride's Diary (1955-56)

Bride's Romances (1953-56)

Love and Marriage (1952-54)

Romantic Marriage (1950-54)

Wedding Bells (1954-56)

Young Brides (1952-56)

4

Screen Dreams

Part 1

THOSE AWFUL TRUTHS: THE TEN BEST FILM COMEDIES ABOUT MARRIAGE

Falling in love is the easy part. *Staying* in love—even merely staying *together*—is the true challenge posed by marriage, and Hollywood films have always been adept at mining this territory for both tears and laughter. Now we turn our jaundiced eyes upon those films that have the courage to show what happens after the honeymoon (both literally and figuratively) is over. Here, then, are our favorite examples of holy—and unholy—matrimony, as served up by Hollywood to America's moviegoers over the years.

1) In THE AWFUL TRUTH (1937)—hailed by film historian James Harvey as "the definitive screwball comedy [and] the purest of all such films"—Cary Grant and Irene Dunne are teamed for the first time as the warring Warriners, who have decided to divorce due to severe (though baseless) attacks of jealousy. While waiting for the decree to become final, Irene wins custody of their wire-hair terrier, Mr. Smith (better known as Asta, from THE THIN MAN), and she and Cary each produce a fiancee who's waiting in the wings. Irene's is a dullard oilman (the hilariously bumbling Ralph Bellamy), while Cary has his eye first on a Southern showgirl (Joyce Compton) with an embarrassing lack of talent, then on a frigid socialite (Molly Lamont). Each undoes the other's constructs of romance—which becomes an agonizing, and agonizingly funny, process—until nothing is left but for them both to admit that they still love each other and will give their matrimony another shot. Leo McCarey, who helped pen the screenplay, won an Oscar for his direction.

McCarey probably would have directed MY FAVORITE WIFE (1940) as well (which he also helped write), had not a serious car accident forced him to relinquish the reins to the young Garson Kanin. Another hysterical romp, the film also stars Grant and Dunne as spouses whose connubial bliss has fallen on hard times. And while some charge WIFE with being a shadow of its glorious predecessor, it's hardly a pale one. Based on the classic tale about Enoch Arden, the film opens with Cary applying before a judge to have first wife Irene Dunne, who was lost after a shipwreck and has been missing for seven years, declared legally dead so that he can wed snooty Gail Patrick. The judge obliges and marries them right in the courtroom—but of course, just as they check into their honeymoon suite, the just-rescued Irene shows up hale and hearty. It turns out she's been shipwrecked on a desert island for the past seven years with strapping Randolph Scott (ironically, Cary's real-life roommate at the time—but that's a whole other story). Cary can't bring himself to tell his new wife about this turn of events, and so is forced to invent an ever more absurd series of excuses as to why he can't consummate their marriage. In the meantime, Irene loses patience with his inability to come clean—he won't even tell their children who Irene really is, the coward!—and so enlists Scott to act as if he'd been her lover on that island the whole seven years, the better to make Cary jealous. That it does, in spades, and Cary finally has to admit to her (and to himself) that it is she with whom he wants to spend the rest of his life.

2) THE PHILADELPHIA STORY (1940) also stars Cary Grant, but here he meets his match in Katharine Hepburn (for whom Philip Barry's play, in which she starred, was written in 1939). Also on hand is James Stewart as a cynical magazine journalist; he and colleague Ruth Hussey have been charged by their tabloid magazine (think *Look*) with the task of covering the impending nuptials of Hepburn's character, an imperious, icy Philadelphia blueblood named Tracy Lord. Cary plays Dexter Haven, an insouciant, dapper, but hard-drinking (and thus, now-exiled) member of Philly society who once was married to Tracy; he's been recruited, for a handsome fee, to help Stewart and Hussey crash the wedding so they can snap exclusive photos for the magazine. (Tracy is to marry the insufferably shallow John Howard— another feeble threat to veteran watchers of romantic comedies.) Stewart is not immune to Tracy's charms, however, and he becomes a formidable rival to Dexter, whose feelings for Tracy have never been wholly extinguished. And, by the final act, Dexter has succeeded in reawakening Tracy's dormant feelings for him.

3) It may not be the absolute best of his indescribably delicious screwball comedies, but THE PALM BEACH STORY (1942) is certainly one of director/writer Preston Sturges's happiest creations. It stars Joel McCrea as a dreamy, pie-in-the-sky inventor and Claudette Colbert as his fed-up wife; she's had her fill of his endless failures, and so has become dillusioned with their marriage. At her wit's end, Claudette takes extreme measures: she leaves McCrea and allows herself to be romanced by prissy millionaire Rudy Vallee, who's on his way to Florida. Joel sets off in hot pursuit, hoping to catch Claudette before some sort of irrevocable action is taken. In the end, their marriage is restored, though in a manner only the wacky Sturges could have cooked up.

THE STARS OF THE YEAR...IN THE PICTURE OF THE YEA

Spencer
TRACY·HEPBURN
Katharine

SPENCE PLAYS
A HAIL FELLOW
SPORTS WRITER
NAMED SAM!

KATE PLAYS
A HIGHBROW
POLITICAL
COLUMNIST
NAMED TESS!

IT'S EITHER LOVE C
'TWIXT SAM AND
and they're good
at both! When they
meet--make eyes--
and make whoopee
- - get set for a
romantic comedy
packed with fun
and surprises all the
way! It tops "The
Philadelphia Story"
for two-fisted en-
tertainment!

LAUGH!
When Spence tries to
teach Kate a little
about sports . . . and
a lot about love!

LAUGH!
When the highbrows
and the mugs rub
elbows at a party!

LAUGH!
When "The Woman
of the Year" marries
. . . and a dozen of
her "public" crash
her honeymoon!

THRILLS and
HEART-THROBS
too! And just wait till
you see the dazzling
gowns Kate wears!

Original Screen Play by
RING LARDNER, Jr. and MICHAEL KANIN
Directed by GEORGE STEVENS
Produced by JOSEPH L. MANKIEWICZ

Metro-Goldwyn-Mayer PICTURE

in
WOMAN OF THE YEAR

A
GEORGE
STEVENS
Production

with
FAY BAINTER
REGINALD OWEN

4) Katharine Hepburn and Spencer Tracy were longtime lovers who, over the course of their twenty-five-year-long affair, denied themselves a marriage certificate because of Tracy's loyalty to his wife and son. Even so, they made a host of absolutely first-rate marital comedies. Perhaps the best of their nine screen collaborations was ADAM'S RIB (1949), that sublime Garson Kanin/Ruth Gordon romp about husband and wife attorneys Adam and Amanda Bonner who end up on opposite sides of an attempted homicide case. Irate wife Judy Holliday has shot and wounded her philandering hubbie, Tom Ewell; Tracy plays the D.A. ready to prosecute her, while Hepburn leaps to the wife's defense, much to Tracy's shock. Naturally, both the actualities and the implications of the case intrude on their marriage, and Spence ends up sleeping on the couch and foraging for his own meals, until Judy's acquittal finally reduces the homefront tensions.

Also worthy of inclusion here is WOMAN OF THE YEAR (1942), the first Tracy/Hepburn team-up, in which he's a hard-boiled sport reporter and she's a haughty political scribe. Their mutual teasing is merciless, but Tracy manages to wear down Hepburn's resistance and win her hand. That gives us the film's unforgettable highlight, when, on the first morning of their wedded bliss, Hepburn totally destroys Tracy's kitchen while trying to brew a humble pot of coffee. (In real life, Tracy prided himself on his coffee-making abilites, so this may have been an in-joke.) Also worth a mention is **WITHOUT LOVE** (1945), based on Philip Barry's 1941 play (which starred Kate on Broadway, just before her romance with Spencer began). It's about a marriage of convenience between an inventor and a widow that, as fate and Hollywood would have it, ultimately blossoms into the real thing.

5) THE THIN MAN (1934) wasn't exactly a screwball comedy—ostensibly, it was a murder mystery based on a novella by Dashiell Hammett. But by the time MGM got done with it, the perfunctory mystery element had receded to the background, leaving the glittering repartee between affectionate spouses Nick and Nora Charles (William Powell and Myrna Loy) front and center. Theirs was a marriage awash in martinis, true, but those olives were floating in a deep reserve of affection, indulgence, and respect. Audiences loved the pair's chemistry, and MGM would make six more Nick and Nora Charles films over the next twelve years. During that time, Powell and Loy were also teamed in a number of other comedies about connubial bliss, including **DOUBLE WEDDING** (1937), **I LOVE YOU AGAIN** (1940), **LOVE CRAZY** (1941), and the classic romp **LIBELED LADY** (1936).

6) A LETTER TO THREE WIVES (1949) is based on an irresistible, if scary, concept: three well-off suburban wives receive identical letters from a woman who informs them that she has run off with one of their husbands. The rest of the film is a series of multiple flashbacks as each wife reexamines her marriage to determine if she herself had planted the seeds of desertion. As the tormented wives, Linda Darnell, Ann Sothern, and Jeanne Crain are excellent, while Kirk Douglas, Paul Douglas, and Jeffrey Lynn are acceptable as the potentially straying hubbies. This film illustrates how quickly the foundation of a marriage can crumble, given a well-placed lever.

7) In **THE FIRST WIVES CLUB** (1996), Goldie Hawn, Bette Midler, and Diane Keaton are splendid as a trio of forty-something ex-wives who panic after learning that one of their college chums committed suicide after her husband had dumped her for a younger woman. Hawn, Midler, and Keaton decide—after a protracted period of wallowing in self-pity—to get revenge on their own smug, philandering husbands, all of whom have realigned themselves with vacuous (albeit gorgeous) younger women. By the time the ex-wives are done, the replacement bimbos have been put out to pasture, the ex-husbands have been mercilessly cut off at the knees, and an organization called the First Wives Club has been founded to help aid and abet victimized wives.

8) Preston Sturges's **UNFAITHFULLY YOURS** (1948) has one of the great comedy concepts of all time: Symphony conductor Rex Harrison, who suspects beautiful wife Linda Darnell of rampant infidelity, fantasizes elaborate scenarios of how he'll exact revenge even as he is conducting before an audience. Of course, it turns out Darnell has been true blue all along, but what a ride we're given along the way. This was remade as a moderately successful film in 1984, with Dudley Moore as the conductor and Nastassja Kinski as his wife.

9) **HANNAH AND HER SISTERS** (1986) turns out to be an affirmation of marriage, unlike most of Woody Allen's other films (see Part 3 below), and so qualifies as a comedy. Michael Caine, Barbara Hershey, Dianne Wiest, and Mia Farrow all score as star-crossed New Yorkers searching for romance, both licit and illicit—particularly Michael Caine as a would-be philanderer. Woody even allows his own (proto-) typically cynical character to find connubial bliss at the film's uplifting conclusion—although not with Mia's character, who ends up with someone else.

10) **FOUR WEDDINGS AND A FUNERAL** (1994) is, admittedly, a British film—but, exercising our infinite editorial latitude, we've selected it as our spe-

REX LINDA RUDY BARBARA
HARRISON · DARNELL · VALLEE · LAWRENCE

Unfaithfully Yours

KURT KREUGER · LIONEL STANDER · EDGAR KENNEDY
ALAN BRIDGE · JULIUS TANNEN · TORBEN MEYER
An Original Screen Play
Written, Directed and Produced by PRESTON STURGES

20th
CENTURY-FOX

cial Foreign Film entry. After all, Andie MacDowell's Carrie, the film's female
protagonist, is an American, and it is her very American philosophy about love
and marriage that dictates the storyline. And as Charles, the perpetual bridegroom, Hugh Grant is wholly endearing, as he longs for the repeatedly
betrothed Carrie even while entering into an engagement or two of his own.
The title literally charts Charles and Carrie's alternating marital activities,
until their stars finally end up in alignment. The film's irrefutable message:
As with most things in life, when it comes to marriage, timing is everything.

Part 2

THOSE CHEATIN' HEARTS:
THE TEN BEST FILMS ABOUT ILLICIT LOVE

1) DOUBLE INDEMNITY (1944) has everyone's favorite murder plot: hot-blooded Barbara Stanwyck tempts stolid Fred MacMurray into knocking off her husband so that the two of them can split the insurance policy. They do the

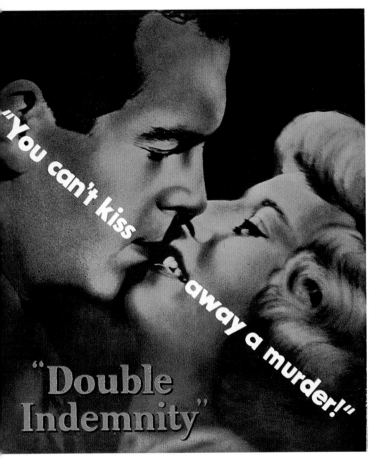

"You can't kiss away a murder!"

"Double Indemnity"

deed, then begin to tear each other apart as mutual distrust and (at least for MacMurray) self-disgust blossom. Meanwhile, Fred's boss (Edward G. Robinson at his querulous best) worries at the logic of the death like a dog with a prime rib bone. In the end, both of the adulterers die—although it's worth mentioning that, in James M. Cain's 1936 novella, they end up doomed to live together while despising each other. The basic plot of *Double Indemnity* would later be shamelessly lifted by Lawrence Kasdan for his neo-noir **BODY HEAT** (1981). Made thirty-seven years later, Kasdan's riff on fatal infidelity does have the advantage of being able to actually show, rather than merely suggest, the steamy, sweaty sex (how about that bathtub tryst!) between sap William Hurt and temptress Kathleen Turner. All of which helps sell the notion that bumping off husband Richard Crenna is not only palatable but wholly inevitable.

2) Michael Douglas's personal triptych of films about straying husbands and wives begins with the 1987 **FATAL ATTRACTION**, in which he meets publishing exec Glen Close at a party, accepts a date, has a wild one-night stand, and then nearly pays for it with his life (not to mention the lives of his family) when Close has an extremely adverse reaction to getting dumped. Next came Douglas's near-infidelity to wife Anne Archer in the 1996 film **DISCLOSURE**, wherein a chain of unpleasant circumstances is set off by rejected temptress Demi Moore, who tries to fob off their near-encounter as a case of sexual harrassment. The Douglas trilogy reached completion in 1998 with A PERFECT MURDER, an imperfect remake of Hitchcock's 1954 quasi-classic DIAL M FOR MURDER (discussed further in Part 4); that earlier version boasts the sublime Grace Kelly, who has the clear edge over the 1998 version's Gwenyth Paltrow.

3) In the 1940 version of THE LETTER (which had also been adapted from Somerset Maugham's play for a rather creaky early talkie in 1929), Bette Davis kills her lover and finagles her way out of a murder charge by lying on the witness stand. But then that letter pops up, and it's the beginning of the end for her. Bette also made a frightening wife the following year in the film of another famous Broadway play, Lillian Hellman's THE LITTLE FOXES.

4) In WAITING TO EXHALE (1995), the four female protagonists don't want to stray—far from it. But each woman becomes a victim of her man's roving eye. Angela Bassett's husband has been cheating on her with his secretary, and, as this adaptation of Terry McMillan's bestseller opens, he coldly dumps her to take up publicly with his paramour. The story continues with Whitney Houston being chased by a married man who, despite his (and her mother's) protestations to the contrary, is cheating on her with his own wife. At the end, the girlfriends find they've got each other, and the heck with the guys.

5) In RED ROCK WEST (1993), J. T. Walsh wants wife Laura Flynn Boyle killed—apparently, he hasn't taken a good look at her lately!—and hires "Lyle, from Dallas" to do the job for $10,000. When dead-broke Nicholas Cage drifts into town, Walsh mistakenly assumes that he is the notorious Lyle, the hitman. Cage agrees to do the job, until he gets a gander at the honey-lipped Boyle, who then persuades him to kill Walsh for her, for double the money. Cage takes her twenty grand and tries to split, but then the real Lyle shows up, and—since

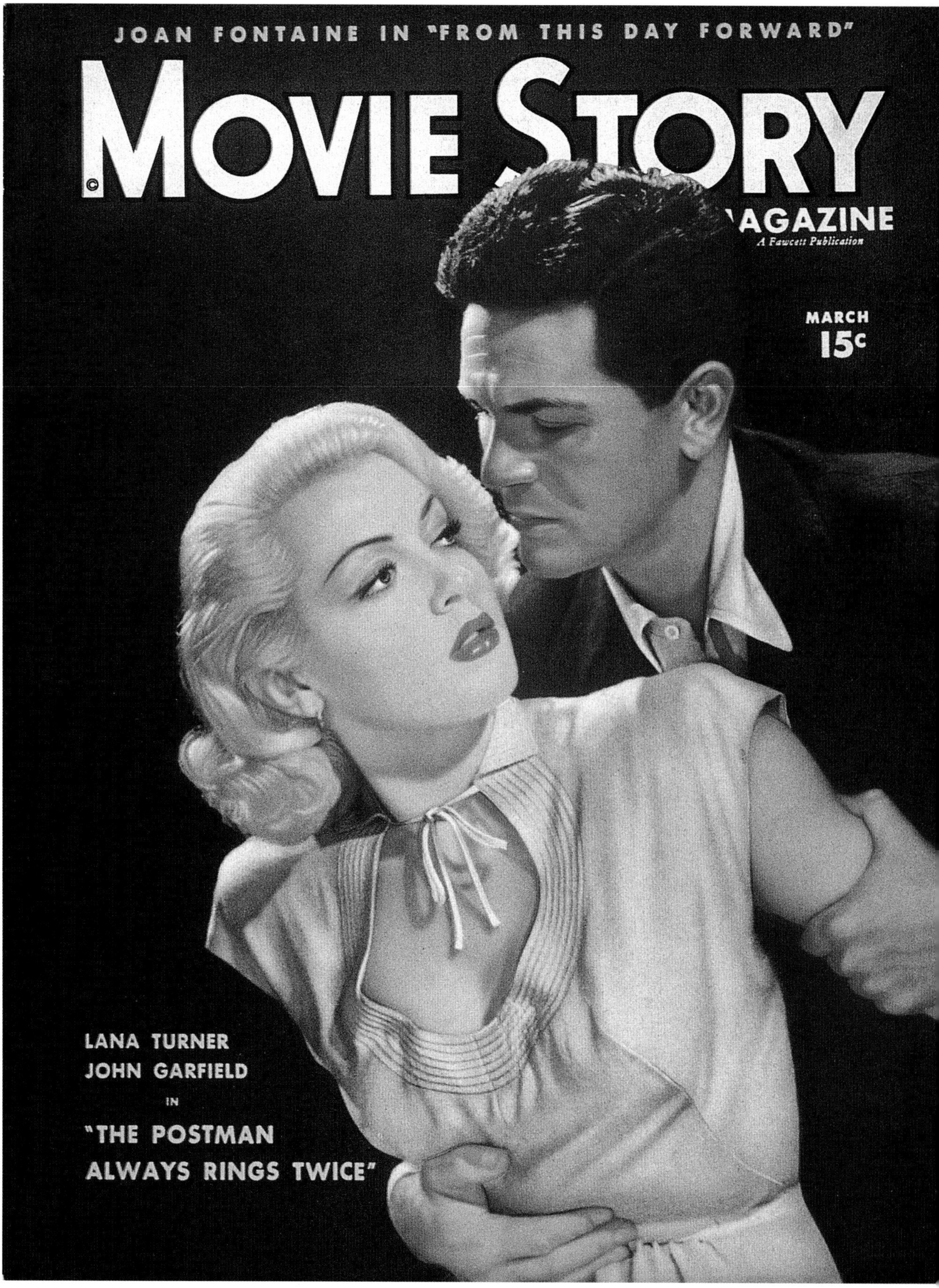

JOAN FONTAINE IN "FROM THIS DAY FORWARD"

MOVIE STORY

MAGAZINE
A Fawcett Publication

MARCH
15c

LANA TURNER
JOHN GARFIELD
IN

"THE POSTMAN
ALWAYS RINGS TWICE"

Lyle is played by Dennis Hopper at his lunatic best—you just know things are going to escalate in a serious way.

6) **INDECENT PROPOSAL** (1993) has a rather farfetched premise: billionaire Robert Redford offers struggling architect Woody Harrelson a million bucks to let him spend one night with his wife, Demi Moore. Woody and Demi discuss the proposal and decide, indecent or not, to let it happen. They then spend the next ninety-plus minutes of screen time sniping at each other over whose lousy idea it was. The embittered couple splits, and Demi accepts the smitten Redford's rather more decent proposal to become his regular girl, while Woody stews in his juices. She serves divorce papers, and Woody signs them with a sneer. Then Woody has an epiphany. As Redford and Demi watch, he donates the million bucks to a charity for the maintenance of a hippopotamus (no, we're not kidding), demonstrating (well after the horse is out of the barn) that he can't be bought. Impressed by this *beau geste*, Redford nobly cuts Demi loose, clearing the way for the reconciliation of the former spouses. Could be based on a true story. But probably not.

7) **HEARTBURN** (1986) has Jack Nicholson and Meryl Streep impersonating that famous real-life couple, writers Carl Bernstein and Nora Ephron, whose once-happy marriage sunders over Bernstein's chronic womanizing. (And she's pregnant, to boot!) At least, that's the way Ephron's screenplay of her best-selling novel lays it out for director Mike Nichols (and us), and she ought to know. When Bernstein submits his own *roman a clef*, we'll report on that, too.

8) In **SCARLET STREET** (1945), timid bank clerk Edward G. Robinson is married to a shrew who doesn't encourage his artistic aspirations. So when he meets beautiful, sympathetic Joan Bennett, it's not surprising that he keeps his unhappy marriage a secret from her. But as their affair develops, he fails to realize that she's just playing him for a sap, setting him up for her hoodlum boyfriend (Dan Duryea, dripping menace) to fleece. Once Robinson sees the light, however, his only way out is an act of violence that leaves him in perpetual purgatory. Nasty stuff, based on Renoir's 1931 **LA CHIENNE**.

9) In **DIARY OF A MAD HOUSEWIFE** (1970), Carrie Snodgrass is driven into the arms of arrogant Frank Langella by the outrageous behavior of smug, hypercritical husband Richard Benjamin and her insufferable spoiled brats. No one in the audience could blame her for a moment. Benjamin gets a nod as well for his

screwed-up husband in the following year's release THE MARRIAGE OF A YOUNG STOCKBROCKER, with Joanna Shimkus now playing his unlucky spouse.

10) James M. Cain's steamy novel about a pair of adulterers who murder to clear the way for their trysting, THE POSTMAN ALWAYS RINGS

TWICE, took twelve years to make it to the big screen. When it did, in 1946, MGM had at least one hand tied behind its back by the restrictions of the Hays Code, which frowned upon films that let their protagonists wallow in illicit lust without paying the piper. And so the rutting, blue-collar characters featured in the novel were transformed by MGM into the brooding John Garfield and the studio's reigning glamour queen, Lana Turner, who dresses throughout in expensive white outfits that belie her character's station in life as the wife of the owner of a roadhouse. But the scene in which they conspire to murder Lana's poor schlub of a husband in cold blood still packs a punch. The 1981 remake, starring Jack Nicholson as the drifter and Jessica Lange as the hot-to-trot wife, wasn't as popular, perhaps because it was ten times more graphic (love that kitchen table covered in flour!).

Part 3

DYSFUNCTION JUNCTION: TEN FILMS THAT WILL PERSUADE YOU NEVER, EVER TO GET MARRIED

1) DAYS OF WINE AND ROSES (1962) is tough stuff, based on a *Playhouse 90* TV drama that starred Cliff Robertson. In this big-screen version, Jack Lemmon and Lee Remick play alcoholic spouses who feed off each other's weakness. The pressures of his job on Madison Avenue drives Lemmon ever deeper into the bottle, and Remick takes up the hobby as a way to keep him company. Soon they're both pathetic lushes, incapable even of caring for their infant daughter. The rueful title song by Henry Mancini won an Oscar.

2) Think Ingmar Bergman set in California's Marin County. That's Alan Parker's SHOOT THE MOON (1982) in a nutshell. In it we find Diane Keaton—always the lover, never the wife, in the many great films she made for and with Woody Allen—making up for lost time, as she provides a finely etched portrait of a married woman on the edge of disaster. Her deeply unhappy husband (Albert Finney, in a blistering performance) is intent on breaking up their fifteen-year marriage by running off with gorgeous (and younger) Karen Allen. At first Keaton is devastated, but once she allows handsome contractor Peter Weller into her life, things brighten up considerably. Of course, her hard-won happiness just plunges the selfish Finney further into despair.

3) It's fair to say that no filmmaker has been more consistently devoted to exploring and deconstructing the state of marriage, American-style, than has Woody Allen over the past twenty-five years. It's a subject near, if not dear, to his heart, and it takes its lumps in films ranging from MANHATTAN (1979) to A MIDSUMMER'S NIGHT'S SEX COMEDY (1982) to CRIMES AND MISDEMEANORS (1989) to MIGHTY APHRODITE (1995). But of his many fine films about wedlock, which one offers the most telling truth? Many fans of Allen opt for the 1979 MANHATTAN. But as good as that film is, its application isn't especially universal—unless the tale of a forty-five-year-old writer who's having an affair with a seventeen-year-old school girl (Mariel Hemingway) after being dumped by a wife who

suddenly discovers that she's a lesbian (Meryl Streep) sounds like someone you know. So let's nod in the direction of two of Allen's other impressive achievements.

HUSBANDS AND WIVES (1992) is not an entirely bleak film; it has its own distinct perspective on the imperatives of both wedlock and adultery, as worked out among cast members Woody, Mia Farrow, Judy Davis, Blythe Danner, Sydney Pollack, and Liam Neeson. But it was released just as Woody's affair with stepdaughter Soon-Yi was scandalizing America, and it was hard to watch objectively. In the deceptively quiet ALICE (1990), Mia Farrow must work up the courage to wander away from her stultifying marriage to philandering, boorish William Hurt. Once she does, she finds the path leads her to the wonderland of an affair with sensitive Joe Mantegna. The upshot: Woody votes Yes on romance, No (most of the time) on marriage. We're betting that he hopes his own life doesn't imitate his art, since he recently tied the knot with Soon-Yi.

4) THE WAR OF THE ROSES (1989) casts Michael Douglas and Kathleen Turner as Oliver and Barbara Rose, a well-off couple on the road to disaster. When we first see them, they are meeting cute—she outbids him for a trinket at an antique auction—and in short order they are marrying cute. But then comes the actual marriage, and they spend the next seventeen years letting it fall apart bit by bit. By the end, things have come to a very ugly pass indeed. Divorce lawyer Danny De Vito (who also directed) narrates the dissolution of the Roses' marriage in all its gory details. With the inexorability of a horror movie, the spouses up the ante with each succeeding mutual insult, until all that remains is Armageddon. A cautionary tale that's enough to make you willingly sleep in the garage for the rest of your days. (And extra points for letting this evolve into an anti-ROMANCING THE STONE, the 1985 smash that first teamed Douglas and Turner as swashbuckling lovers.)

5) WHO'S AFRAID OF VIRGINIA WOOLF? (1966) is almost as much of an ordeal to sit through as it must have been to perform. Based on the 1962 Edward Albee play, this is 129 minutes of unabated marital venom between college professor George and the college president's daughter, Martha, played by what was then the world's most famous wedded couple, Richard Burton and Elizabeth Taylor. George Segal and Sandy Dennis, as a nominally better-adjusted couple, end up fastening their seatbelts for a bumpy ride when George and Martha invite them back for a nightcap after a faculty party. This Mike Nichols film was a sensation in its day, not the least because Liz and Dick were famed as real-life donnybrookers, having captured the world's imagination ever since Burton stole Liz away from Eddie Fisher (whom *she* had stolen away from Debbie Reynolds—oh, yeah, you already know all that.) It spelled Oscar for the courageously blowsy Liz—her second, after the "sympathy" Oscar she received in 1961 for BUTTERFIELD 8, when everyone was fearful she might die of pneumonia.

6) In THE REF (1994), cat burglar Denis Leary makes the mistake of breaking in on perpetually squabbling young marrieds Kevin Spacey and Judy Davis. He finds that even tying them up can't slow down their insufferable, bitter bickering. This could have been a black comedy classic, were there some way of not making the audience just as sick of Spacey and Davis as Leary quickly becomes.

7) IN NAME ONLY (1939) pairs the indefatigable Cary Grant with Kay Francis, who plays a selfish, social-climbing monster who doesn't have an honest emotion in her body—unless it's envy. Bound to her, Cary naturally responds to vibrant widow Carole Lombard, who, aware of his situation, patiently waits in the wings, hoping against hope that he'll one day be free to join her. After much back and forth, of course he does.

CLARK GABLE'S PREVIEW OF "GONE WITH THE WIND"

MOVIE STORY

MAGAZINE
(Reg. U. S. Pat. Off.)

A FAWCETT PUBLICATION
MOVIE STORY
10¢

OCTOBER
N S C

Carole Lombard
and Cary Grant

MOVIE STORIES STARRING
GARY COOPER, JEAN ARTHUR
JAMES STEWART, ALICE FAYE
CHARLES BOYER, IRENE DUNNE
CAROLE LOMBARD, CARY GRANT

8) In Francis Ford Coppola's PEGGY SUE GOT MARRIED (1986), Kathleen Turner plays a forty-three-year-old who's trapped in an unhappy marriage with boorish, unfaithful Nicholas Cage, her old high-school sweetheart. Then she passes out at her 25th high school reunion and wakes up back in her senior year; now she gets to live out the widely shared fantasy of returning to high school to relive events with her adult knowledge intact. There she finds the seventeen-year-old version of the self-centered Cage already trying to dominate her life, but she also finds that she has an option she missed the first time around: an adoring brainiac classmate who figures out what Peggy Sue has done and proposes marriage to her. Should she divert the course of her life to avoid disaster? Or accept the hopelessly flawed Cage yet again and pray for a better result? Suspenseful, but more than a little depressing.

9) In NEW YORK, NEW YORK (1977), Robert De Niro is a cocky sax player named Jimmy Doyle, and Liza Minnelli is a big band singer named Francine Evans. Jimmy chases Francine, Jimmy gets Francine, Jimmy weds Francine. Soon Jimmy has knocked up Francine, and once he starts playing around on her, he deservedly gets dumped. Then Jimmy's pride prevents him from getting back with Francine when she extends an olive branch. De Niro's Jimmy is so self-destructive you often feel like letting De Niro's Jake La Motta administer him a good thrashing.

10) TWO FOR THE ROAD (1967) finds Audrey Hepburn (nearing the end of her film career) and Albert Finney (a few years removed from his Oscar for TOM JONES) flashing back over the key events of their now-dissolving marriage. There's the almost accidental manner in which they met, their courtship, their spats, their affairs. Although the couple reconciles by film's end, the precarious nature of their twelve-year union has been exposed, leaving us uncertain what might happen to them as time goes by. An uncomfortable portrait of a romance that has run out of petrol, thanks to Frederic Raphael's unsparing screenplay.

20th Century-Fox presents

AUDREY HEPBURN

(STAR OF "TOM JONES")

ALBERT FINNEY

THEY MAKE SOMETHING
WONDERFUL
OUT OF BEING ALIVE!

columns

es)

¾ inches

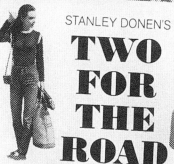

STANLEY DONEN'S

TWO FOR THE ROAD

with
ELEANOR BRON · WILLIAM DANIELS · CLAUDE DAUPHIN · NADIA GRAY
produced and directed by STANLEY DONEN · written by FREDERIC RAPHAEL
music - HENRY MANCINI · Panavision® Color by DeLuxe
ORIGINAL SOUNDTRACK ALBUM AVAILABLE ON RCA VICTOR RECORDS

Suggested For Mature Audiences

Part 4

YOU'RE NOT PARANOID—
YOU'RE JUST MARRIED!

It's not really paranoia if someone is really trying to kill you—right? So when that someone turns out to be a husband or a wife, what's a spouse to do? Case in point: Alfred Hitchcock's REBECCA (1940), adapted from the popular novel by Daphne du Maurier. Attention, Joan Fontaine—the moral of this Oscar-winning concoction is obvious: Don't marry a widower (even dashing Larry Olivier) whose dear departed is jealous of you. Joan got to demonstrate her paranoia chops again in Hitchcock's 1941 SUSPICION—but, the original novel notwithstanding, husband Cary Grant wasn't really attempting to harm her (his glowing glass of milk notwithstanding). A more extreme case of marital menace is GASLIGHT (1944), in which Charles Boyer really *does* try to drive spouse Ingrid Bergman insane, and almost succeeds (this was based on a 1940 British film that now is rarely seen). Also in 1944, the low-budget WHEN STRANGERS MARRY finds the young Robert Mitchum helping newlywed Kim Hunter extract herself from the clutches of husband Dean Jagger, whom she believes may be a murderer. (And, guess what: she's right!)

THE TWO MRS. CARROLLS (1947), earlier a successful Broadway play, finds Barbara Stanwyck in peril from husband Humphrey Bogart, who—she learns a bit belatedly—has the unpleasant habit of painting macabre portraits of his wives before slaying them. Loretta Young isn't much better off in CAUSE FOR ALARM (1950), in which she discovers that hubby Barry Sullivan is a murderous psychopath. The shoe is on the other foot in the 1953 melodrama NIAGARA, which stars Joseph Cotton and Marilyn Monroe as spouses who can't wait to get rid of each other—permanently. When Cotten realizes that Marilyn is trying to kill him, he trumps her by strangling her and kidnapping Jean Peters, a honeymooning bride who surely is going to have second thoughts about the efficacy of marriage for some time. And then we have Grace Kelly being menaced by either a mysterious stranger or husband Ray Milland in Alfred Hitchcock's 1954 3-D thriller DIAL M FOR MURDER. That plot was essentially lifted for the 1960 potboiler starring Doris Day, MIDNIGHT LACE, in which

NEW HIT PICTURES IN THRILLING STORY FORM

MOVIE STORY MAGAZINE

MOVIE STORY 10¢   JUNE

Joan Fontaine
Cary Grant in
"Before the Fact"

BEFORE THE FACT STARRING JOAN FONTAINE, CARY GRANT
LOVE CRAZY STARRING MYRNA LOY AND WILLIAM POWELL
ONE NIGHT IN LISBON WITH MADELEINE CARROLL, FRED MacMURRAY
AFFECTIONATELY YOURS WITH MERLE OBERON, DENNIS MORGAN

husband Rex Harrison is trying to both drive her nuts *and* kill her (better to be safe than sorry).

One of our personal faves is the 1958 sci-fi shocker I MARRIED A MONSTER FROM OUTER SPACE, in which newlywed Gloria Talbott gradually becomes aware that hubby Tom Tyron has been possessed by an alien, as have all the other husbands in town—a problem that plagues many New Jersey communities to this very day. But the all-time champ in the category of marital paranoia may well be Roman Polanski's 1968 film of Ira Levin's neo-gothic bestseller, ROSEMARY'S BABY. Mia Farrow is at her most fragile as a young wife whose ambitious husband (John Cassavetes, at his demonic best) has literally made a deal with the devil to further his acting career. More recently, screengoers enjoyed the spectacle of an utterly terrorized (but still adorable) Julia Roberts having to fake her own death to avoid abusive (and compulsively neat) husband Patrick Bergin in SLEEPING WITH THE ENEMY (1991). He stalks Julia as if auditioning for a role in one of the "Halloween" pictures, so you can guess his fate.

In THE EDGE (1997), billionaire Anthony Hopkins can't shake the feeling that his young, gorgeous wife (supermodel Elle Macpherson) is carrying on an affair with a handsome photographer (Alec Baldwin). By the time Hopkins learns that he's right, he and Baldwin are stranded in the Alaskan wilderness being chased by a huge Kodiak bear (played convincingly by "Bart"). And in the quasi-update of Hitchcock's DIAL M FOR MURDER,

now titled A PERFECT MURDER (1998), Michael Douglas is plotting to have his straying wife (Gwenyth Paltrow) murdered—by the very lover (Viggo Mortensen) with whom she's cuckolding him! Some daydreams about our spouses simply never go out of fashion.

Part 5

SIXTY-SIX FLICKS ABOUT FIDELITY, AND OTHER MARITAL MOTIFS

The subject of marriage has always been a staple of Hollywood movies, dating back to the first days of the industry. Many of those early dramas and comedies have since been lost to the ages, however, making it nigh impossible to view such provocatively titled silent film fare as *The Matrimaniac* (1916), *A Looney Honeymoon* (1918), *Don't Change Your Husband*, *Winning His Wife*, and *The Probation Wife* (all from 1919). Nonetheless, many of the movies from the sound era spanning the last seventy-odd years remain in circulation, some on video, some on premium cable channels. We present them here as much for their tantalizing titles as any merit they might possess as cultural artifacts:

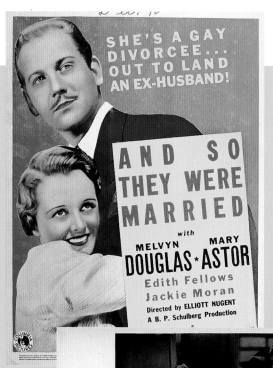

1) AND SO THEY WERE MARRIED (1936): Melvyn Douglas and Mary Astor have each been widowed, but they don't take much of a shine to each other when they end up wintering at the same inn. Neither do their respective kids. But, somehow, the title tips us off that those little obstacles shall be overcome.

2) ALIMONY (1949): Just in case it doesn't work out, might as well be prepared.

3) AND BABY MAKES THREE (1949): Estranged couple Robert Young and Barbara Hale may need to reconcile, as it seems that Robert knocked her up just before they separated. Only one problem—she's now engaged to marry Robert Hutton. Oh, well—like they say, father knows best.

4) BAREFOOT IN THE PARK (1967): Neil Simon's Broadway success becomes a mild essay in wedded wackiness on the screen, with fresh-faced Robert Redford and Jane Fonda (yeah, it was over thirty years ago!) as newlyweds having compatibility problems. It seems he's too straightlaced while she's a pre-Woodstock free spirit. Then, one day, Redford gets plastered and agrees to go running barefoot through Central Park as a symbol of his newly unfettered spirit, saving their marriage for all time.

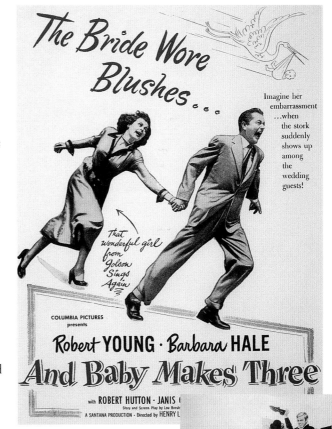

5) Tim Burton's morbid comedy **BEETLEJUICE** (1988) has a whole bunch of great jokes; one of the best is that dead couple Alec Baldwin and Geena Davis have a better marriage than the live couple (Catherine O'Hara and Jeffrey Jones). And BeetleJuice's (Michael Keaton) wedding ceremony with Winona Ryder is truly one for the ages.

6) THE BISHOP'S WIFE (1947): Loretta Young and David Niven are trying to raise money for a new church; they're also less than happily married, so angel Cary Grant pays them a visit to help set things right. But what is to happen when Cary finds himself attracted to Loretta? Remade in 1997 with Whitney Houston, Denzel Washington, gospel music, and a new title: **THE PREACHER'S WIFE**.

7) BLONDIE (1938-1950): While Chic Young's comic strip has been running since 1930, Columbia's twenty-eight B-movies about the battling Bumsteads, with Penny Singleton and Arthur Lake in the title roles, constitute a pretty impressive thirteen-year run of their own. The installments typically revolved around a single

crisis in the Bumstead's marriage: BLONDIE MEETS THE BOSS, BLONDIE ON A BUDGET, BLONDIE'S HOLIDAY, BLONDIE'S ANNIVERSARY, and so on.

8) BLUEBEARD'S EIGHTH WIFE (1938): "He married in haste and repeated with pleasure!" So this Ernst Lubitsch confection was advertised. Gary Cooper takes Claudette Colbert as his eighth bride—the first seven having taken him to Reno, and the cleaners, to the tune of $50,000 settlements per divorcee. But Claudette promises to be a horse of a different color, if only Gary can figure out how to tame her.

9) BOB & CAROL & TED & ALICE (1969): Talk about time capsules: director/writer Paul Mazursky's ode to free love (read: wifeswapping) needs carbon dating. But as the eponymous title characters, Natalie Wood and Robert Culp (as couple number one: the sophisticates) and Dyan Cannon and Elliot Gould (as couple number two: the converts) have enough star appeal to keep things from getting altogether risible.

10) THE BRIDE OF FRANKENSTEIN (1935): "The Monster Wants a Mate!" cried the advertising for this superb sequel. Of course, in the end, the creature (brilliantly played by Boris Karloff) was greeted after the ceremony with blushing bride Elsa Lanchester's happy response—a great, big HISSSSSSSS!

11) BRIDE OF THE GORILLA (1951): Hulking jungle-plantation owner Raymond Burr gets to marry foxy Barbara Payton, but can't enjoy himself, as he seems to be turning into an ape. Freud would've gotten a big chuckle out of this baby.

12) BRINGING UP FATHER (1946): Joe Yule and Renie Riano made a series of low-budget adaptations of George McManus's famous comic strip about those avatars of marital dysfunction, Jiggs and Maggie. Jiggs is the ne'er-do-well husband, Maggie his battleaxe of a wife, with her rolling pin always at the ready. Others in the series include JIGS AND MAGGIE IN COURT and JIGS AND MAGGIE IN SOCIETY

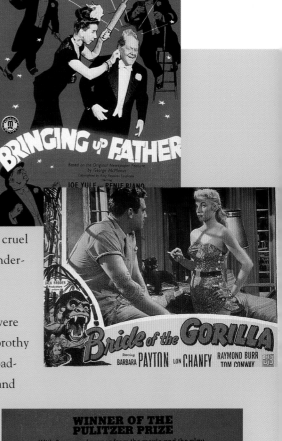

13) CAT ON A HOT TIN ROOF (1958): This is a rather tepid film version of Tennessee Williams's 1955 play about a monumentally unhappy married couple living in the Southern mansion of rich "Big Daddy" Burl Ives. Paul Newman is the gorgeous but alcoholic and sexually dysfunctional son of the cruel Ives, while his loving wife, the voluptuous Elizabeth Taylor, is understandably frustrated with Newman's bitterness and impotence.

14) CLAUDIA (1943) and **CLAUDIA AND DAVID** (1946) were based on the popular novels by Rose Franken. In the first film, Dorothy McGuire essays the role (which she had already performed on Broadway) of the newly married, wholly innocent Claudia, whose husband (Robert Young) helps her learn about life. In the sequel, the young couple moves to the 'burbs, has a baby, and faces other, equally intimidating challenges. We've all been there.

15) DIVORCE AMERICAN STYLE (1967): Dick Van Dyke and Debbie Reynolds long to be divorced—but once they are, things don't improve as they'd hoped. Written by Norman Lear, who a few years later would unleash his historic marital sitcom, *All in the Family,* upon television audiences.

16) DODSWORTH (1936): Wealthy industrialist Walter Huston is trapped in a loveless marriage with social-climbing wife Ruth Chatterton, so when he falls for a lovely widow (Mary Astor) while on vacation, he despairs of ever being able to pursue a romance with her. But then Chatterton is caught out having an affair with a young gigolo, leaving Walter and Mary free to pursue their happily unmarried destiny together.

17) DOUBLE WEDDING (1937): Powell and Loy moonlighting from their roles as Nick and Nora Charles—now he's an avant-garde painter, she's a dress designer. Ostensibly

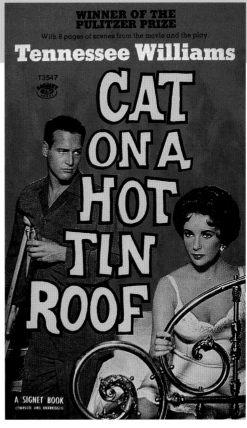

they're trying to marry off Loy's sister (Florence Rice), but—true to form—they end up getting married themselves.

18) EMERGENCY WEDDING (1950): Larry Parks is jealous of the time his doctor wife (Barbara Hale) spends with her patients. It's a remake of the 1941 film YOU BELONG TO ME, which had Henry Fonda and Barbara Stanwyck in the same situation, with the same humdrum results.

19) EVERY GIRL SHOULD BE MARRIED (1948): Cary Grant is a marriage-shy bachelor doctor who tries to fend off the interest of Betsy Drake, who would soon become Cary's real-life wife. She's also sought by that perennial number-two suitor Franchot Tone, who tries but fails to gum up the works.

20) THE EX-MRS. BRADFORD (1936): Having charged him with non-payment of alimony, Jean Arthur blackmails unreliable ex-husband William Powell, a coroner, into letting her help him solve a murder. When the feuding and fencing is all over, they're back in each other's arms, renewing their vows.

21) FATHER OF THE BRIDE (1950): Irascible Spencer Tracy tries to be a good dad to daughter Elizabeth Taylor, who is preparing for marriage to Don Taylor. But, oh, is his patience ever tested! Still, you gotta love the guy, especially when he tries to cream fussy caterer Leo G. Carroll. With Joan Bennett as his saintly wife. Remade in 1991 with Steve Martin as the father, Diane Keaton as his wife, and Martin Short as the insufferable caterer.

22) THE GAY BRIDE (1934): Carole Lombard plays a gold-digging showgirl who agrees

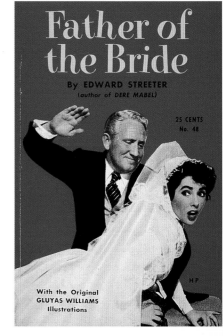

to marry gangster "Shoots" Magiz for riches and security. Then she falls in love with bodyguard Chester Morris, and things get complicated.

23) GONE WITH THE WIND (1939): Sure, some people would put this cherished film in a category all its own. But to us, **GWTW** is just another flick (albeit, a very long one) about a woman who marries a guy because someone else wants him, and who then squanders his true love for her. By the time she sees the light, it's too damn late. You already know that it's Vivian Leigh doing the squandering here, and that it's roguish Clark Gable whom she's squandering.

24) THE GRASS IS GREENER (1960): Yet another of Cary Grant's inimitable excursions into the shoals of matrimony. Here his wife is Deborah Kerr, and hunky Robert Mitchum is the guy testing her faithfulness. (If any actor is a credible challenge to Cary, Mitchum is that guy.) Cary, in the meantime, finds his own vows put to the test by attractive neighbor Jean Simmons.

25) A GUIDE FOR THE MARRIED MAN (1967): Walter Matthau thinks he wants to learn how to cheat on his wife, the beautiful Inger Stevens. But after studying a variety of increasingly absurd strategies, he decides he's happy enough where he is.

26) HARRIET CRAIG (1950): Joan Crawford anchors the third go-round of George Kelly's melodramatic play *Craig's Wife*, which was previously filmed in 1928 and 1936. Wendell Corey now has the thankless task of acting as Joan's long-suffering punching bag . . . er, husband . . . who isn't allowed to smoke in the house, set down a magazine, or otherwise disrupt Harriet's perfectly antiseptic home. (His breathing and bathroom privileges are not disclosed.)

27) THE HEARTBREAK KID (1972): Charles Grodin is hilarious as a bridegroom whose Florida honeymoon with Jeannie Berlin (daughter of Elaine May, who directed this) is derailed when he spies young, luscious Cybill Shepherd on the beach and, encouraged by her flirtations, becomes obsessed with winning her. He dumps bride Berlin in one of the all-time brutal (but hilarious) kiss-offs, then follows Cybill to her home in Minneapolis, where she's a college student with a huge Nordic boyfriend. Understandably, she has little interest in this pushy Jewish nut from New York. Her wealthy dad (Eddie Albert) would move heaven and earth to get Grodin to leave his daughter alone, but somehow Grodin's perseverance triumphs, and Cybill agrees to marry him after all. But once he has his golden girl in hand, Grodin demonstrates signs of cold feet once again.

28) HE MARRIED HIS WIFE (1940): "He" is Joel McCrea, who moves heaven and earth to get ex-wife Nancy Kelly a new husband so that he can cease his alimony payments. The title tips you off as to how it all ends up.

29) HIRED WIFE (1940): Roz Russell marries boss Brian Aherne for reasons of appearance, but Virginia Bruce has her own designs on him. And then Roz actually falls in love with the smug sap. The rest takes about eighty minutes to sort out.

30) HIS GIRL FRIDAY (1940): Just before making MY FAVORITE WIFE and THE PHILADELPHIA STORY, Cary Grant performed in this Howard Hawks classic. Here Cary's a hard-boiled newspaper editor, who realizes he can't afford to let feisty ex-spouse Rosalind Russell—his star reporter—go though with her plans to wed the long-suffering Ralph Bellamy. So Cary intervenes as only Cary can, and by the end of this frenetic picture, she's returned to his arms. Adapted from the Hecht-MacArthur screenplay for THE FRONT PAGE—but you won't find the protagonists married in any of the other stage or screen versions.

31) I MARRIED A COMMUNIST (1949): A sad tale from another time. Robert Ryan, who foolishly belonged to a communist cell in his youth, is blackmailed by a bunch of modern-day Commie thugs into letting them infiltrate the docks, exposing the thousands of men who toil there to their noxious philosophy. His wife, Laraine Day, gradually learns to her horror that Ryan is under their sway. Worse still, her younger brother, John Agar, has allowed himself to be seduced by Red strumpet Janis Carter. Agar is defenstrated, but with the help of Laraine's loyalty, Ryan manages to outwit the gang—leaving the docks free for more politically correct forms of mob infiltration.

32) I MARRIED A WITCH (1942): Gorgeous witch Veronica Lake was burned at the stake hundreds of years before by a Salem witchhunter, whose descendant in 1942 turns out to be Fredric March. Now March is engaged to marry Susan Hayward, but—much to her own surprise—Lake eschews her plan for vengeance, instead bewitching March so she can have him for herself. Twenty years later, this charming conceit would supply the premise for the TV series *Bewitched*.

33) I WANT A DIVORCE (1940): Dick Powell and Joan Blondell, real-life spouses since 1936, here play newlyweds who are having second thoughts. Eventually, Powell and Blondell experienced their own second thoughts, divorcing in 1945.

34) I WILL, I WILL . . . FOR NOW (1976): The year before she made **ANNIE HALL**, Diane Keaton starred opposite Elliot Gould in this frenetic farce about a divorced couple who try to repair the damage by sampling everything from marriage counseling to attending a sex clinic.

35) JUST MARRIED (1928): Ruth Taylor and Lila Lee both want to wed the original Harrison Ford. They should have waited for our modern-day version to arrive.

36) KISS ME, KATE (1953): Cole Porter's popular Broadway musicalization of *The Taming of the Shrew* was brought to the silver screen—in 3-D, no less!—starring Howard Keel as a Broadway actor about to star as Petruchio in the play by Shakespeare, with Kathryn Grayson as the ex-wife he must call on to play opposite him as Katherine "the shrew"; Ann Miller played Keel's girlfriend, whom he has cast to play Katherine's sister, Bianca. By the end of the production, the ex's are reunited in "real" life as on stage. Compare it to the inventive version of the play filmed in 1967 by Franco Zeffirelli, with real-life spouses Liz Taylor and Richard Burton duking it out as passionate mates Katherine and Petruchio—truly a case of life imitating art. **SHREW** was also filmed in 1929, starring the then-reigning king and queen of Hollywood, Douglas Fairbanks and Mary Pickford—but that version seems to be lost to the ages.

37) LET'S GET MARRIED (1937): Ida Lupino and Ralph Bellamy want to, all right. But it's never that easy, is it?

38) LOVE CRAZY (1941): Powell and Loy yet again, this time as a warring couple on the verge of divorce. To forestall that fate, Powell feigns insanity, figuring that Myrna wouldn't be cruel enough to leave him while he's in such a fragile state. Fortunately for him, the film is a comedy.

39) LOVE STORY (1970): "Preppy millionaire" Ryan O'Neal and vapid Ali McGraw meet cute, marry cute, and then she dies—well, not cute, exactly, but she certainly looks pretty glam as she wastes away from some unnamed but ever-so-fatal disease. And to think, his sourpuss dad (Ray Milland, now glazed ham) frowned on their union. One of the year's biggest hits—and Oscar-nominated, fer the lovva Pete!—from the Erich Segal bestseller. Taps into the fantasy of never having to say you're sorry that you're getting bored.

40) MADE FOR EACH OTHER (1939): Jimmy Stewart and Carole Lombard are married and struggling with medical bills they can't meet. Jimmy's mother, Lucille Watson, throws gasoline on the fire, but the young marrieds manage to persevere.

41) MARRIAGE IS A PRIVATE AFFAIR (1944): Lana Turner marries serviceman John Hodiak just before he's due to be shipped overseas, selfishly figuring that she'll have a few years to herself before really settling down. Imagine her panic when Hodiak's orders are changed, forcing Lana to undertake the duties of wifehood immediately—and constantly.

42) THE MARRYING KIND (1952): Aldo Ray and Judy Holliday, on the verge of divorce, relive the painful events that brought them to such a pass.

43) MONKEY BUSINESS (1952): Cary Grant (the most married guy on the silver screen!) and wife Ginger Rogers take a fountain-of-youth serum which rejuvenates their flagging marriage—

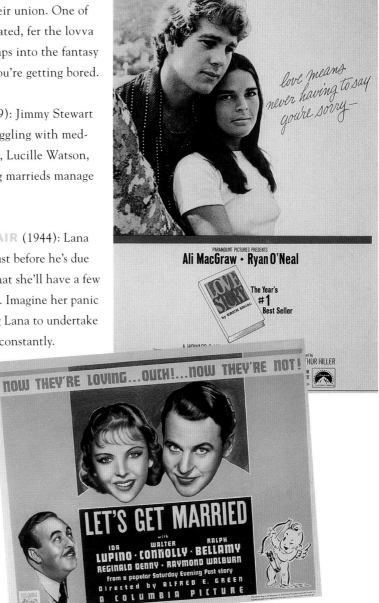

love means never having to say you're sorry—

PARAMOUNT PICTURES PRESENTS
Ali MacGraw · Ryan O'Neal

LOVE STORY by ERICH SEGAL

The Year's **#1** Best Seller

NOW THEY'RE LOVING...OUCH!...NOW THEY'RE NOT!

LET'S GET MARRIED
with
IDA · WALTER · RALPH
LUPINO · CONNOLLY · BELLAMY
REGINALD DENNY · RAYMOND WALBURN
From a popular Saturday Evening Post story
Directed by ALFRED E. GREEN
A COLUMBIA PICTURE

though not without unexpected side effects, one of them named Marilyn Monroe.

44) MR. AND MRS. SMITH (1941): The ineffable Carole Lombard and the affable Robert Montgomery live—and battle incessantly—on Park Avenue, until they discover that their marriage isn't legal. (So what was Alfred Hitchcock doing, making a screwball comedy?)

45) MODEL WIFE (1941): Dick Powell and Joan Blondell must marry secretly, lest Joan's boss dismiss her. So, how long can she keep their nuptials a secret?

46) THE MOON'S OUR HOME (1936): Erstwhile spouses Henry Fonda and Margaret Sullavan, who were actually married in 1931 and divorced in 1933, may have had some fun performing in this screwball yarn about the jealousy between a Hollywood actress and her novelist/explorer husband, whose separate claims to fame nearly scuttle their marriage.

47) NIAGARA FALLS (1941): Because every marriage has to start somewhere.

48) OUR WIFE (1941): Melvyn Douglas and Ruth Hussey are engaged, but ex-wife Ellen Drew isn't letting go gracefully, behavior with which Hussey understandably takes issue.

49) THE PERFECT MARRIAGE (1946): Loretta Young and David Niven are bored with each other after ten happy years of marriage. Can they rediscover the spark in time to avoid divorce? You needn't even ask.

50) PHFFFT! (1954): Jack Lemmon and Judy Holliday get a divorce, then realize they were happier when united.

51) REPENT AT LEISURE (1941): Starring Kent Taylor and Wendy Barrie. Our favorite movie title.

52) REVERSAL OF FORTUNE (1990): Jeremy Irons and Glenn Close are Claus and Sunny von Bulow, wealthy socialites whose arid, pro forma marriage becomes tabloid fodder across the nation when Sunny lapses into a coma from an overdose of insulin. Claus is charged with attempted murder, and into the fray comes Boston lawyer Alan Dershowitz (Ron Silver). He tries to overcome his personal repulsion for the reptilian Claus, who suspiciously has found himself an attractive new girlfriend; ultimately, Dershowitz mounts a brilliant strategy (well, this is adapted from his own book about the case) that reverses the jury's murder indictment. But neither Dershowitz nor the viewer ever learns whether Claus was, in fact, responsible for his wife's permanent plight.

53) SHE MARRIED AN ARTIST (1937): Now she's in trouble. Starring John Boles and Luci Deste, whoever she is.

54) THAT UNCERTAIN FEELING (1941): Merle Oberon gets the hiccups whenever the word "marriage" is mentioned, and it gets mentioned plenty, since she's married to Melvyn Douglas. Can a shrink help? Directed with aplomb by the great Ernst Lubitsch.

55) THEY WANTED TO MARRY (1937): Betty Furness and Gordon Jones want to, and by gum, they do. We hope they're satisfied.

56) TOO MANY HUSBANDS (1940): Remember the plot of the 1940 screwball classic MY FAVORITE WIFE? Well, here it is again, in another picture made the same year. Jean Arthur, thinking she's a widow, marries Melvyn Douglas, but then first husband Fred MacMurray turns up very much alive. From a Somerset Maugham play.

57) TOPPER (1937): Yet another goodie from the fertile mind of Thorne Smith. Cary Grant and Constance Bennett are the impossibly attractive, fun-loving, but—alas!—recently deceased couple George and Marion Kerby,

who are brought back as spirits to advise and aid henpecked Roland Smith, before wife Billie Burke can grind him into sawdust. Made into a pretty good television series in 1953.

58) TRUE LOVE (1989): Hilarious account of a young Bronx Italian couple preparing for their nuptials. That is, *she* (Annabella Sciorra) is preparing; he (Ron Eldard) is doing his best to ignore the whole thing, hanging out with his buds and hoping he'll wake up to find that it's all been just a bad dream. But as so many of us have learned, marriage is all too real.

59) TRUE ROMANCE (1993): Comic-book-store clerk Christian Slater falls for quasi-hooker Patricia Arquette, decides he wants to marry her, and does after a nail-biting showdown with her lethal pimp (Gary Oldman at his most frighteningly kinky). Their honeymoon to LA is derailed, though, when the suitcase full of cocaine that Slater accidentally absconded with turns out to belong to the Mob. They want it back; he sees it as their nest egg. Sweet in its own demented way, after one has hosed off the blood, this twisted film is screenwriter Quentin Tarantino's idea of a romantic comedy.

60) TURNABOUT (1940): Another great Thorne Smith notion: Carole Landis and John Hubbard exchange bodies, or souls, reversing their roles and learning how the other half truly lives. If this had starred Cary Grant instead of Hubbard, it might have been a classic.

61) THE WAY WE WERE (1973): Waspy conservative Robert Redford and Jewish radical "Babs" Streisand as politically, culturally and iconocly incompatible man and wife? Well, that's why, after a protracted courtship, they get divorced and stay that way.

62) A WEDDING (1978): Robert Altman directed this noisome hodge-podge about a wedding involving two upwardly mobile families. But it does offer the only screen teaming of Desi Arnaz, Jr., Pam Dawber, and Lillian Gish.

63) WEDDING PRESENT (1936): Cary Grant and Joan Bennett are newspaper reporters whose mutual attraction is derailed when Cary is promoted to editor over her. She accepts George Bancroft's marriage proposal, but Cary isn't ready to slink away; he disrupts their wedding ceremony and kidnaps Joan until she agrees to come to her senses. Whenever we try that, it never works.

64) THE WEDDING SINGER (1998): Adam Sandler is a modestly talented singer who scrapes by fronting a band that performs at—you guessed it—suburban weddings. He falls into despair when his fiancee dumps him a week before his wedding, but rallies when he falls in love with winsome Drew Barrymore—who has hired him to sing at her wedding. But it's okay—she loves him too, and he saves her from marrying a "total jerkoff." You won't want to get married for several weeks, at least, after viewing this jaundiced comedy.

65) WE'RE NOT MARRIED (1952): Six couples learn that their marriage ceremonies weren't conducted legally, and must reexamine their motivation for doing it in the first place. Some stick with it, and some breathe a sigh of relief.

66) WICKED WIFE (1954): We know the type. Here it's the tawdry Beverly Michaels.

Our Twelve Favorite True Tales of Matrimony from the Confession Magazines

1) "Marriage of Necessity," from *True Experiences*, March 1941.

2) "I Was a Selfish Husband" from *True Confessions*, July 1940.

3 & 4) "I Was a Wife Without Shame" and "My Mother-in-Law's Revenge," both from *True Story*, December 1952.

5 & 6) "Confessions of an Army Wife" and "It Might Have Been a Good Marriage," both from *True Story*, March 1941.

7 & 8 & 9 & 10) "I Was an Unmarried Mother" and "When My Husband Strayed" and "My Mad Elopement" and "I Married for Money," all from *True Story*, October 1936.

11) "I Hated My Marriage!" from *True Story*, July 1954.

12) "Unwanted Bride: The Story of a Strange Marriage," from *True Experiences*, May 1940.

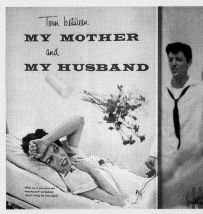

Torn between
MY MOTHER
and
MY HUSBAND

The two people I loved most glowered at each other in black rage. I cried, "Why can't you get along? If you love me, why are you wrecking my life?"

LYING BRIDE

DOUBLE-LENGTH story of a wife's greatest mistake

I gave my husband all my heart's love—all my soul's fire and all the perversed lies my mind could invent

I hated my marriage!

I married Carl, vowing to be the best wife, the best mother I could be. I tried. But he didn't help me. When he began to act as if he hated the sight of me, I felt rejected, unwanted. I started to hate him, too...

• She couldn't bear to have anyone know she was an unloved wife. At first she had been hurt, then she battled it out with herself. She couldn't leave him even when she knew she was being deceived because—

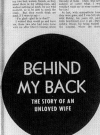

BEHIND MY BACK

THE STORY OF AN UNLOVED WIFE

True Experiences

MAY 10¢

BOOK LENGTH TRUE NOVEL

LOVE THIEF
THE STORY OF THE MAN MY SISTER MARRIED

5

Songs for the Simple Life

Part 1

TEN TIME-TESTED TUNES ABOUT GETTING, BEING, OR UN-BEING MARRIED

1) "WE'VE ONLY JUST BEGUN" by The Carpenters (1970): Everyone's favorite song-to-get-married-by, this shamelessly sappy ditty details the deliriously happy first days of a newlywed couple. "So much of life to learn/We'll start out crawling and learn to walk . . . White lace and promises/A kiss for luck and we're on our way." Bon voyage!

2) "TO THE AISLE" by The 5 Satins (1957): Things were simple in the Fifties, weren't they? "First a girl and a boy/Get together . . .You say, Darling, please put me on trial/As we walk, our hearts beat together/While each step/Takes us closer/To the aisle." Brace yourself, kids! There's a whole lot more to come!

SPOTLITE ON
THE CARPENTERS

Karen was born Karen Anne Carpenter on March 2, 1950, in New Haven, Connecticut.

She is five feet and four inches tall, weighs about 118 pounds, and has long dark brown hair and brown eyes. She recently changed her hair style—and doesn't she look groovy?

She loves to play the drums—and is excellent at it!

Karen and her brother were recently named Musical Group Of The Year **by the American Guild of Variety Artists—an award which will be presented to them on the Ed Sullivan** Entertainer Of the Year **special.**

Her favorite singing groups all start with B's—the Beatles, the BeeGees, the Beach Boys and Bread!

She loves old college musical shows.

Bright red is her favorite color.

She loves to eat—some of her fav foods are grapefruit, shrimp and chocolate ice cream.

Bowling, baseball and drag racing thrill her!

On dates, she likes to see musical groups in concert—natch!

She and her brother last year received **three Grammy Awards**—Best New Vocal Group, Best Album and Best Single of the Year.

She and Richard and their parents now live in Downey, California.

Karen's cozy bedroom is filled to overflowing with her stuffed animal collection.

Richard Lynn Carpenter was born on October 15, 1946, in New Haven, Connecticut.

He is six feet tall, weighs 175 pounds, has hazel eyes and blond hair.

His parents' names are Harold and Agnes. Karen and Richard are their only children.

Richard is very **shy with girls!**

Richard drives a Maserati and hopes to race it some day.

Besides singing background and playing the piano and organ, Richard arranges, writes and orchestrates music.

His fav foods are steak and spaghetti—in fact, he likes almost everything except avocados and artichokes.

He is not much of a sports fan.

He would like to act in a comedy skit.

He and Karen record for A&M records and they have five gold singles—for Close To You, We've Only Just Begun, For All We Know, Rainy Days and Mondays **and** Superstar. **Their two LPs,** Close To You **and** Carpenters, **have sold over a million copies each.**

Richard and Karen will soon be making a concert tour of the Orient and Australia.

You can write to Richard and Karen at Box 4375, Downey, California 90241.

3) "CHAPEL OF LOVE" by The Dixie Cups (1964): Originally recorded by the Ronettes on their 1963 debut album, this infectious tune was composed by the legendary Ellie Greenwich/Jeff Barry/Phil Spector team of tunesmiths. It would prove to be one of the only songs by an American group (The Dixie Cups were a trio of teenagers from New Orleans) to hit number one on America's pop charts in the first half of 1964—the height of the British Invasion. Its lilting refrain is still heard every hour or two on Oldies radio: "Goin' to the chapel and we're/Gonna get married/Yes, I really love you, and we're/Gonna get married/Goin' to the chapel of love . . .Today's the day/We say 'I do'/And I'll never be lonely again."

4) "WEDDING BELL BLUES" by The Fifth Dimension (1969): "For the devotion in my heart/I take no bows/But am I ever going to hear/Those wedding vows?" This clever Laura Nyro composition had been a minor chart success for her in 1967, but it hit number one for The Fifth Dimension in November 1969, featuring a plaintive lead vocal by Marilyn McCoo. She was at the time engaged to fellow Fifth Dimension-member Billy Davis, Jr. "But kisses and sighs/Won't carry me through/Until you marry me, Bill/I've got the wedding bell blues/Please marry me, Bill!" And we're happy to report that, in real life, Billy did.

5) "THE WEDDING SONG (THERE IS LOVE)" by Paul Stookey (1971): Posing the musical question, "Well, then/What's to be the reason/For becoming man and wife?" this elegant, quasi-religious ballad quickly became the anthem of couples tying the knot in the early Seventies. We heard it at an outdoor wedding held in a garden in Shaker Heights, Ohio, on August 24, 1974 (less than two weeks after Richard Nixon left office), and we're happy to report that the marriage is still going strong.

6) "ME AND MRS. JONES" by Billy Paul (1972): An extramarital affair that the narrator guiltily admits he is powerless to break off is the leitmotif of this soulful ballad, which hit number one on the U.S. charts. "Me and Mrs. Jones, Mrs. Jones/We got a thing goin' on/And it's much too strong/To try and stop now . . . Now you'll go your way/And I'll go mine/We'll meet tomorrow/Same place, same time." Actually, he doesn't sound all that guilty.

7) "HUSBANDS AND WIVES" by Roger Miller (1966): "It's my belief that pride/Is the chief cause in the decline/In the number of husbands and wives." All too true. Happily, we, your editors, checked our pride at the door.

8) "BAND OF GOLD" by Freda Payne (1970): Far and away the best pop tune about the nightmarish pressure of the honeymoon night that—eventually—each and every one of us must confront. As the song's patently virginal narrator tells it, she freaked out after the lights went down that first night of married life, obliging her new husband to leave the bedroom in disgrace. Her explanation: "You took me/From the shelter of a mother/I had never known/How to love any other/But that night, on our honeymoon/We stayed in separate rooms." Now the repentant narrator reflects, "Now that you've gone, all I have are the dreams I hold/Of a band of Gold/And the memory, of what love could be/If you were still here with me." It is to weep.

9) "WIVES AND LOVERS" An up-tempo ditty sung by jaunty Jack Jones that had something to do with the 1963 movie of the same name. But what we really like are the lyrics: "Hey, little girl/Comb your hair, fix your makeup/Soon he will walk through the door/Don't think because/You've a ring on your finger/You needn't try anymore/For wives should always/Be lovers too/Run to his arms/The moment he comes home to you/He's almost there . . ." Were truer words ever sung?

JANET LEIGH · VAN JOHNSON · SHELLEY WINTERS · MARTHA HYER in
Wives and Lovers
RAY WALSTON · JEREMY SLATE   A HAL WALLIS Production
Directed by JOHN RICH · Screenplay by EDWARD ANHALT · A PARAMOUNT RELEASE

10) And, to help *untie* the knot, we submit **"YOU DON'T BRING ME FLOWERS"** by Barbra Streisand and Neil Diamond (1978), a bitter, blow-by-blow litany of complaints by each spouse that contrasts their happy salad days together with the impending end of their marriage. Originally, Streisand and Diamond had each recorded the song on their own separate albums, but an imaginative Louisville deejay named Gary Guthrie spliced the versions together and broadcast his call-and-response synthesis, creating a demand from listeners for a version they could buy in a store. Columbia dutifully had the stars record a new version, which hit number one and was nominated for numerous Grammy awards. But DJ Guthrie had to sue CBS to receive compensation for his brilliant idea, making this the only song about a marriage to end up in court with the lawyers.

Archive Photos

Part 2
ROCK'N'ROLL'S MOST HARMONIOUS MARRIED COUPLES

1) JOHN LENNON AND YOKO ONO got married on March 20, 1969, and their bedroom "sleep-in" to protest the Vietnam war made headlines the world over. But their unconditional (or so it seemed) devotion to each other drove a wedge between John and the other Beatles, no doubt helping to accelerate the band's breakup. John and Yoko managed to remain in the spotlight throughout the Seventies, culminating with their ambitious *Double Fantasy* album, a reaffirmation of their union made even more poignant by its release just after Lennon's assassination in December 1980.

Archive Photos

2) JOHN AND MICHELLE PHILLIPS, of The Mamas and Papas. It was California Dreamin', for a while.

3) SONNY AND CHER. The beat went on, and so did they—individually. But their couple-hood would be immortalized for posterity in the unintentionally hilarious made-for-TV bio-drama *Sonny and Cher*, broadcast by ABC during February sweeps in 1999.

4) JAMES TAYLOR AND CARLY SIMON. "You Belong to Me"—and then, one day, they didn't. At least not to each other.

5) THE CAPTAIN AND TENNILLE (Daryl Dragon and Toni Tennille), auteurs of "Do That to Me One More Time," "Muskrat Love," and other odes to marital ecstasy.

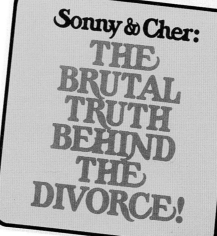

6) CAROLE KING AND GERRY GOFFIN: Songwriters with classics to their credit like "Will You Love Me Tomorrow," "The Loco-Motion," "Take Good Care of My Baby," "Up on the Roof," "One Fine Day," and "(You Make Me Feel Like) A Natural Woman," among many others. Divorced in 1968.

7) IKE AND TINA TURNER. With one of the rockiest marriages on record, they certainly rated their own biopic, and this time the moviemakers got it right: the 1993 critical success *What's Love Got to Do With It?*, starring Angela Bassett and Laurence Fishburne.

Archive Photos

8) PAUL AND LINDA MCCARTNEY—the yin to the yang of the intentionally outrageous John and Yoko. Paul and Linda at

Archive Photos

first blush seemed too goody-two-shoes for the cynical Sixties—but as that decade gave way to the touchy-feely Seventies and the every-man-for-himself Eighties, their union seemed less cloying and more righteous. (Though we could have done with a bit less of their strident endorsement of PETA-style issues, which we sometimes suspected Linda of roping Paul into endorsing.) When Linda died of breast cancer in 1998, the rock press offered an outpouring of sympathy—and then went on to pan her posthumous album, *Wide Prairie*.

9) KURT COBAIN AND COURTNEY LOVE. He was from the band Nirvana, she from Hole. The charismatic grunge rockers met in 1991, got married (with Cobain decked out in green flannel pajamas) on February 24, 1992, and had a baby later that year. But the union was torn asunder when Cobain commited suicide on April 6, 1994. Since that time, there have been whispers (including the 1998 documentary film Kurt and Courtney) that Love somehow conspired in her husband's death. She vehemently denied all such accusations.

10) GEORGE JONES AND TAMMY WYNETTE. Yeah, we know they don't qualify as rock'n'roll, but let's not pick nits here. This self-destructive pair of country music superstars, having already recorded such duets as "The King and Queen of Country Music," got married in 1969 (although Jones was slapped with a $100,000 alienation-of-affection suit by Tammy's erstwhile husband). The well-publicized ups and downs of their marriage were reflected in several of their hit records, including the number-one hit "We're Gonna Hold On." But Jones's addiction to alcohol and cocaine put too great a strain on the marriage, and it ended in 1974. Even after their divorce, though, George and Tammy continued to record together, topping the charts with tales of marital woe like "Golden Ring."

Years later, George would still be trying to kill himself, most recently with his near-fatal auto accident in February of 1999. And, even after her death in 1998, Tammy managed to stay in the headlines as well—three of her four daughters noisily challenged the validity of her cause of death (a blood clot in her lungs was the official finding), launching a $50 million wrongful-death lawsuit that was still being adjudicated at this writing.

FIFTY GREAT, NEAR-GREAT, AND PRACTICALLY FORGOTTEN TELEVISION SHOWS ABOUT THE INSTITUTION OF MARRIAGE

1) THE ADDAMS FAMILY [1964-1966, ABC]

A mordantly humorous portrayal of one of our era's most passionate marriages, that of Morticia (the sultry Caroline Jones) and Gomez (John Astin, whose leer was incomparable); based on Charles Adams's cartoons for *The New Yorker*.

2) ALL IN THE FAMILY [January 1971-September 1983, CBS]

Archie and Edith Bunker (Carroll O'Connor and Jean Stapleton), the *lumpenprole* of Queens, surely had their roots in Ralph and Alice Kramden of *Honeymooners* fame, but the issues the show dealt with—abortion, bigotry, homosexuality, menopause—made it uniquely topical for the time. *All in the Family* was at its best when its main issue was the marriage of the Bunkers, with the faintly

abusive, always abrasive Archie finding the initially meek Edith more and more willing to stand up to him with each passing season. As a counterpoint was the marriage of quasi-hippies "Meathead" Mike Stivic (Rob Reiner) and the Bunkers' daughter, Gloria (Sally Struthers), who lived with the Bunkers for several years before ultimately finding their own home. Counterculture or not, their marriage evinced plenty of problems, too.

3) AN AMERICAN FAMILY [1973, PBS; 12-part documentary]

The poor Louds of Santa Barbara. When they were chosen to be the real-life subjects of a national public television documentary, they surely must have pinched themselves, celebrating such one-in-a-million good fortune. But, once the cameras rolled, they were quickly exposed to be a severely troubled family on the verge of disintegration. At the center of their entropy was the marriage of Bill and Pat Loud, which unraveled like a cheap suit from episode to episode (some 300 hours of footage were shot over seven months by producer Craig Gilbert), until Pat Loud filed for divorce somewhere between the eighth and ninth installments.

4) BEWITCHED [1964-1972, ABC]

A great concept: *I Married a Witch* transposed to an upscale Connecticut suburb, with Elizabeth Montgomery as the supernaturally gifted Samantha Stevens. To the dismay of her meddling, haughty mom Endora (the veteran character actress Agnes Moorehead), "Sam" married New York advertising executive Darrin Stephens (Dick York, initially; Dick Sargent inherited the role in the 1969 season) and swore to herself never to employ her witchly powers. But, somehow, each week she found a good reason to break that vow. What God hath brought together, let no mother-in-law's spell cast asunder!

5) THE BOB NEWHART SHOW [1972-1978, CBS]

Maybe it wasn't the sort of marriage we would have enjoyed being locked into for half a century, but there was something about the gently bickering relationship between Newhart (who played neurotic Chicago shrink Bob Hartley) and Suzanne Pleshette (as acerbic wife Emily) that stuck to one's ribs in a pleasant way.

6) THE BRADY BUNCH [1969-1974, ABC]

You already know the premise: widower Robert Reed, dad to three sons, marries widow Florence Henderson, who's mother to three daughters. We were just old enough not to understand how anyone could tolerate this fluff, let enough relish it—but, hey, we used to think *The Monkees* was a hoot, so what do we know?

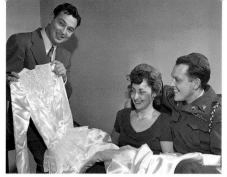

7) BRIDE AND GROOM [1951-1953, CBS; 1953-1954 & 1957-1958, NBC]

Originally a popular radio series, this moved to television because the excitement simply couldn't be contained in any other medium: couples getting married, live, in front of a studio audience! Our only question—what genius took this off the air?!?

8) BRIDGET LOVES BERNIE [1972-1973, CBS]

Might have been ahead of its time. Or behind it—the premise about a rich Irish girl (Meredith Baxter) marrying a poor Jewish boy (David Birney) dates back to the 1911 stage perennial *Abie's Irish Rose*. But we like it because Baxter and Birney fell in love and got married during the show's single season. So what if they later got divorced? She kept his name, didn't she?

9) THE BURNS AND ALLEN SHOW [1950-1958, CBS]

Let's recognize this minimalist production in honor of George Burns and Gracie Allen's long-running, real-life marriage, rather than anything that actually happened on the show. (Did anything ever happen on the show?)

10) CIVIL WARS [1991-1993, ABC]

A nice concept: The lawyers (Mariel Hemingway and Peter Onorati) specialize exclusively in domestic relations cases. (That gives us the nifty title.) But it would have been more fun if the partners weren't just dating. Turn it into an *Adam's Rib* for the Nineties, we say.

11) THE COSBY SHOW [1984-1992, NBC]

Bill Cosby was one of this hugely successful series' co-creators; in it, Coz played Brooklyn obstetrician Cliff Huxtable, and his feisty wife, an attorney, was played by Phylicia Rashad. And then there were all those kids, with whom we fortunately needn't concern ourselves here. Cosby was the biggest hit of the Eighties, and did much to advance family values, promoting a healthy relationship between equal spouses. But those warm and fuzzy values can get cloying in a hurry—we always preferred less wholesome fare, like *Manimal*.

12) DHARMA AND GREG [1997- , ABC]

A slightly less innocent updating of *Barefoot in the Park*, with

Archive Photos

Archive Photos

straight-arrow Thomas Gibson married to way, way-out neo-flower-child Jenna Elfman, much to the horror of their respective sets of parents (one set straight WASPs, the other Jewish hippies). The humor is strained and the mating is noisy and faintly nauseating—but this is what passes for the Lubitsch touch in the Nineties, God help us.

13) THE DICK VAN DYKE SHOW [1961-1966, CBS]
"ROB!!" That plaintive cry of Mary Tyler Moore to hubbie Dick Van Dyke was a hallmark of what may have been the most appealing television marriage of the Sixties. Let's put it this way: No matter how cockamamie each week's plot was (and they were usually as stupid as the plots of most Sixties TV shows), you always could imagine Rob and Laura getting into bed with each other once everything was straightened out—and not just to sleep.

14) THE DONNA REED SHOW [1958-1966, ABC]
Wholesome Donna Reed and stolid Carl Betz played the Stones, with support from Shelley Fabares as daughter Mary and former Mouseketeer Paul Petersen as wiseguy son Jeff. Lots of family hugger-mugger, and little focus on the marriage of the Stones, as was typical then for this kind of family sitcom. Still, you wouldn't have minded if they were *your* mom and dad.

15) EIGHT IS ENOUGH [1977-1981, ABC]
Betty Buckley arrived *in media res* to help save widower Dick Van Patten from the permanent doldrums, and their characters got married on November 9, 1977. If that weren't enough excitement, two pairs of the kiddies got hitched in the fall of '79. And you thought nothing ever happened during the Carter administration!

16) FAMILY TIES [1982-1989, NBC]
Forget Michael J. Fox's first licensed entry into the scenery-chewing business. Isn't it more important that the show gave Meredith Baxter Birney a chance to play a wife again, this time to Michael Gross, as Elyse and Steven Keaton of Columbus, Ohio? Even if their credentials as former hippies seemed less than impeccable, there have been less convincing boob-tube marriages. If only NBC hadn't allowed Michael J. Fox to shanghai the show, Birney (who looked like his barely older sister) and Gross might have been given something more interesting to do.

17) FAMILY [1976-1980, ABC]

Serious but very entertaining stuff, about a Pasadena family confronted week after week with internal challenges. James Broderick and Sada Thompson had a marriage that was tested again and again, not least by their divorced, single-mom daughter, Meredith Baxter Birney, who moves back in with them. (Look—we aren't the ones who keep casting her in these things, we're just reporting it!)

18) FATHER KNOWS BEST [1954-1955, CBS/1955-1958, NBC/1958-1962, CBS]

Not that mom (Jane Wyatt) didn't have a good head on her shoulders, too, but it was usually left to somber Robert Young (well, he was playing an insurance agent) to set straight the little problems besetting the Anderson clan of Springfield (Ohio? Massachusetts? Or maybe it's the one Homer Simpson calls home). A success on radio for five years before moving to television, this was the template for all those other fondly remembered family sitcoms.

19) THE GOLDBERGS

[1949-1951, CBS/ 1952-1953, NBC/1954, DUMONT/1954-1955, syndicated] A long-running radio success about a loving, but bickering, Jewish family in the Bronx that bounced around from network to network during the time of the Magna Carta.

20) HE AND SHE [1967-1968, CBS]

Richard Benjamin plays a New York City cartoonist and real-life wife Paula Prentiss is a Traveler's Aid worker in this short-lived sitcom, which featured some very colorful friends and neighbors (Jack Cassidy, Hamilton Camp, Kenneth Mars, Harold Gould).

21) HERE COME THE BRIDES [1968-1970, ABC]

Set in the Washington woods of the 1870s, this knock-off of *Seven Brides for Seven Brothers* starred teen idol Bobby Sherman and idol-to-be David Soul, though most of the cast was made up of girls, girls, girls (ostensibly imported from New Bedford, Massachusetts).

22) HOME IMPROVEMENT [1991-1999, ABC]

Tim Allen reached superstardom in this amiable vehicle, in which he plays the host of the Detroit television show "Tool Time." Patricia Richardson is his knowing wife, and what she knows is: he's not really

an expert on much of anything, concerning tools or anything else. For a couple of years, bombshell Pamela Anderson played "Tool Time"'s resident bombshell, in a marvel of
life imitating art.

23) HOW TO SURVIVE A MARRIAGE
[1974-1975, NBC; daytime serial]
All daytime dramas by definition include multiple storylines
about husbands and wives and their respective lovers, so we
included this one just for the evocative title.

24) HUSBANDS, WIVES, & LOVERS [1978, CBS]
Five couples living in southern California examine their marriages when one of the couples announces their separation. We
must have blinked during this show's three-month run in '78.

25) I LOVE LUCY/THE LUCY-DESI COMEDY HOUR
[1951-1957/1957-1960, CBS]
Springing from the template of the 1949 CBS Radio series My *Favorite Husband*, which starred film comedienne Lucille Ball and B-movie specialist
Richard Denning, *I Love Lucy* was given the call to be developed for television.
That was fine with Ball, on the condition that her husband since 1940, Cuban
bandleader and B-movie actor Desi Arnaz, be cast in place of Denning. The
rest, as they say, is history, so familiar has the lore of Lucy and Desi Ricardo and
their phlegmatic neighbors, Fred and Ethel Mertz (the equally wonderful
William Frawley and Vivian Vance) become. And so it has remained for nearly
a half century, thanks to the magic of those endless reruns.

26) I MARRIED JOAN [1952-1955, NBC]
Joan Davis, who owned the series, sorta played herself, and Jim Backus (whom
we remember better for his stalwart comic turns on *The Adventures of Dobie
Gillis* and *Gilligan's Island*) was cast as her husband, Judge Bradley Stevens.

27) IT PAYS TO BE MARRIED [1955, NBC; game show]
A short-lived daytime Q&A show on which married couples faced off against
other married couples for dough-re-mi. (Might as well get something out of the
old ball and chain!)

28) IT TAKES TWO [1969-1970, NBC; game show]
Dodgers broadcaster Vin Scully was the odd choice to host this competition among three celebrity couples and their spouses; just as oddly, the questions were restricted to the field of mathematics.

29) IT TAKES TWO [1982-1983, ABC]
Patty Duke Astin is an assistant D.A., while hubby Richard Crenna is a surgeon who resents her entering into the workforce. It didn't seem very interesting at the time, but now we'd give it another whirl, knowing their teenage daughter and son were played, respectively, by future megastars Helen Hunt and Anthony Edwards.

30) THE JACKIE GLEASON SHOW (THE HONEYMOONERS) [1952-1959, 1961-1970, CBS]
There has never been a blue-collar married couple on television who could trump the Ralph and Alice Kramden of Jackie Gleason and Audrey Meadows, and we respectfully submit that there never will be. (Please, *Roseanne* us no *Roseanne's*.) It's fondly remembered and watched in reruns even today, more than forty years after the peak broadcast years of *The Honeymooners* (which began as a skit within the framework of *The Jackie Gleason Show* in the early '50s, then graduated to a stand-alone show in the 1955, '56 and '57 seasons). And do we ever love booming out that "To the moon, Alice!!" line to our wives while brandishing a menacing fist. Of course, since neither of our wives is named Alice, they don't pay the least bit of attention.

Archive Photos

31) THE JEFFERSONS [1975-1985, CBS]
This is one of the most successful spinoffs ever, with Archie Bunker's former neighbors moving from Queens to "a deluxe apartment in the sky" in Manhattan's Upper East Side. Sherman Hemsley was George Jefferson, the monumentally irascible husband to the forbearing, forgiving Louise (Isabel Sanford).

32) KING OF THE HILL [1996- , FOX; animated]
A small town Texas family is held together—just barely—by the not-quite dysfunctional marriage of Hank and Peggy Hill. Hank, a redneck by birth but

not by nature, works for a natural gas company, and patronizes Peggy shamelessly. The great thing about the show is, Hank eventually does begin to develop a sense of shame. The deal with son Bobby, one of television's most original characters, would require a book of its own.

33) THE LIFE OF RILEY [1949-1950, 1953-1958, NBC]

After a successful run as a radio series from 1944 to 1949, the program moved to TV, with Jackie Gleason assigned the title role of perpetual loser and hapless family man Chester A. Riley (a riveter by trade) and his wife Peg (Rosemary DeCamp). Veteran film character actor William Bendix, who had starred in the original radio series, took over as Riley when the show resumed airing after a two-year hiatus, with Marjorie Reynolds cast as his wife.

34) LITTLE HOUSE ON THE PRAIRIE [1974-1982, NBC]

Michael Landon played wise, warm dad Charles Ingalls, and Karen Grassle was his wise, warm wife, Caroline, in this long-running adaptation of Laura Ingall Wilder's wise, warm series of books about her parents, set in 1870s Walnut Grove, Minnesota. Even their kids weren't so bad. Ah, the 1870s!

35) LOVE ON A ROOFTOP [1966-1967, ABC]

Judy Carne and Peter Duel played a newlywed San Francisco couple who live in a tiny apartment with—you guessed it—easy access to the roof. Rich Little and Barbara Bostock were their older, but rarely wiser, married neighbors.

36) LOVE STORY [1955-1956, CBS; game show]

A daytime quiz show that pitted newlywed couples against each other with a trip to Paris as the stakes. Sounds cool, but we were four years old then and watching Howdy Doody.

37) MAD ABOUT YOU [1992-1999, NBC]

As Paul and Jamie Buchman, Paul Reiser and Helen Hunt were (for a time, anyway) a convincing embodiment of contemporary wedlock—the neurotic, New York City variety. More than most

sitcoms, this series spent a large portion of its screen time directly on critical contemporary issues about marriage, including how hard it is to arrange to actually sleep together. And how hard it is to sleep, period, when someone's sleeping next to you.

38) MAKE ROOM FOR DADDY (THE DANNY THOMAS SHOW)
[1953-1957, ABC/1957-1964, CBS]
Danny Thomas played a version of himself named Danny Williams, nightclub comedian and singer par excellence, with Jean Hagen as his wife, Margaret, and a couple of kids underfoot. In 1956, Hagen left the series, and Danny became a widower (with the show changing its name to *The Danny Thomas Show*). But during the year, his character met a widowed nurse played by Marjorie Lord, and by the end of the '56-'57 season they had married.

39) THE MARRIAGE [1954, NBC]
Real-life spouses and classy stage stars Hume Cronyn and Jessica Tandy slummed briefly on this summer sitcom about a New York couple named Ben and Liz Marriot.

Archive Photos

40) MARRIED: THE FIRST YEAR [1979, CBS]
It didn't last a year, as the title optimistically promised . . . barely a month, in fact. But then, not every marriage lasts that long, either. (Just ask Ernest Borgnine about his seven-day marriage to Ethel Merman!) Leigh McCloskey and Cindy Grover played the young marrieds who faced a different challenge every week. As do us old marrieds.

41) MARRIED . . . WITH CHILDREN [1987-1998, FOX]
All about the battlin' Bundys, with Ed O'Neill as the rude, crude, socially unacceptable Al, a shoe salesman, and Katey Sagal as the spandexed, non-Jewish princess Peg. Most episodes, regardless of plot, are glued together by Al and Peg's relentless, remorseless stream of cutting insults, which might as well have been scripted by Don Rickles. An ode to mutual contempt that has managed to entertain more than it has offended for over a decade now.

42) MAUDE [1972-1978, CBS]
Yet another successful spinoff from *All in the Family*, this sitcom cast Bea Arthur as the caustic, ultra-liberal Maude Findlay (Edith Bunker's cousin) and Bill Macy as

Archive Photos

RADIO-TV MIRROR

MARCH

EXCLUSIVE
JAY STEWART
●
THE TRUTH ABOUT
JAN MURRAY

Ozzie and Harriet Nelson

NANCY COLEMAN
Valiant Lady

DAVE GARROWAY
Fascinating Fellow

PATSY CAMPBELL
Second Mrs. Burton

her loving, if understandably cowed, fourth husband, Walter. Adrienne Barbeau's presence as her divorced, live-in daughter Carol gave Maude plenty of opportunity to spout off on the subject of marriage.

43) MCMILLAN AND WIFE [1971-1977, NBC]
Rock Hudson played San Francisco Police Commissioner Stewart McMillan, and pert Susan St. James was his plucky, sexy wife, Sally. It was a Nick and Nora Charles–flavored detective show—or would have been, had Hudson had a tenth the charm of William Powell. After St. James left the series, Rock carried on one last season as a widower.

44) NEWHART [1982-1990, CBS]
Not as fondly recalled as *The Bob Newhart Show* (see page 118), but Newhart had its simple charms. This time Bob plays Dick Loudon, an author who moves to Vermont with his wife (the too-bland Mary Frann) to become an innkeeper. Probably the best of Newhart's vehicles; if nothing else, the supporting cast here was his funniest. But Suzanne Pleshette's vim and vinegar was needed to balance this equation.

45) THE NEWLYWED GAME
[1966-1974, ABC/1977-1980, syndicated/1985-1990, syndicated]
Smarmy as the day is long, this series, hosted by Bob Eubanks, managed to transcend the hot-and-bothered state of its dim-bulb contestants by provoking situations guaranteed (experienced viewers knew) to set them at each other's throats with can openers and baling wire, sex or no sex. A masterpiece of its kind.

46) [THE ADVENTURES OF] OZZIE AND HARRIET [1952-1966, ABC]
Marriage? What marriage? This long-running series somehow managed to wholly avoid any semblance of interest in, or comment on, the lives of its nominal stars as husband and wife. Instead, the kids (David and Ricky) and their mild misadventures dictated the "plot" of each week's episode. Be glad your dad didn't hang around the house all day, ostentatiously drinking root beer, while you were growing up!

47) PETE AND GLADYS [1960-1962, CBS]

Harry Morgan was Pete Porter and Cara Williams played his ditzy wife Gladys in this harmless waste of a half hour. (Well, whoever said that marriage had to be interesting?)

48) ROSEANNE [1988-1997, ABC]

Perhaps the least appealing marriage in the annals of television history was that of Roseanne and Dan Conner (Roseanne Barr and John Goodman), an endlessly contentious blue-collar couple who struggled noisily against the world, each other, their three kids, and anything else you had to offer. Many loved this program, and it made Roseanne (nee Barr) into a star of the first magnitude—for a while, anyway. Certainly John Goodman, as Roseanne's husband, was a paragon of *lumpenprole* virtue. But, on the whole, we preferred Philadelphia.

Archive Photos

49) THE SIMPSONS [1990- , FOX; animated]

Not since the days of *The Honeymooners* has television offered such an acutely rendered portrait of a marriage—that of Marge and Homer Simpson, the creations of cartoonist Matt Groening. We particularly liked the episode in which Marge and Homer discover they can only get into the mood for lovemaking when they undertake the act in public—one location was a miniature golf course. But there are a dozen other episodes that are just as universally applicable. Somehow, what began as a wee bit of a joke has developed into the most profound show of our time. Heck, to us, it's the best darn TV show about marriage *ever*, even when it isn't about marriage.

Archive Photos

50) THIRTYSOMETHING [1987-1991, ABC]

This is ground zero for marital dramas by, about, and for baby-boomers. Heavy on the issues (and heavy on everything else, too) the show covered every aspect of an Eighties-something yuppie marriage: illness, infidelity, job stress, parenting stress, home renovation stress—and those were the lighter episodes. Still, for fans of angst and anomie, this one was hard to beat. Bonus points for real-life spouses Ken Olin and Patricia Wettig agreeing to play husband and wife to other actors (Mel Harris and Timothy Busfield, respectively).

Epilogue

JUST IN CASE IT DOESN'T WORK OUT AFTER ALL . . .

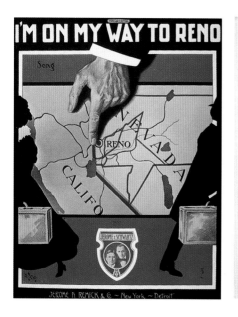

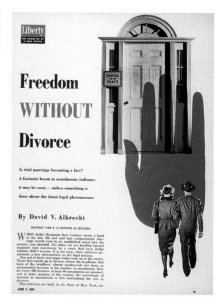

Bibliography

Berman, Louis A. *Proverb Wit & Wisdom*. New York: Perigee, 1997.

Compiled by the Editors of CineBooks. *The Movie Guide*. Third Edition. New York: Perigee, 1998.

Harvey, James. *Romantic Comedy in Hollywood, from Lubitsch to Sturges*. New York: Knopf, 1987.

Katz, Ephraim. *The Film Encyclopedia*, 2nd Edition. New York: Harper Perennial, 1994.

Maltin, Leonard. *Leonard Maltin's Movie & Video Guide*, 1999 Edition. New York: Plume, 1998.

McNeil, Alex. *Total Television*. 4th Edition. New York: Penguin, 1997.

Nickens, Christopher. *Elizabeth Taylor: A Biography in Photographs*. New York: Doubleday/Dolphin, 1984.

The Oxford Dictionary Book of Quotations. Third Edition. New York: Oxford University Press, 1979, 1980.

Sikov, Ed. *Screwball: Hollywood's Madcap Romantic Comedies*. New York: Crown, 1989.

Spada, James. *Grace: The Secret Lives of a Princess*. New York: Doubleday, 1987.

Tripp, Rhoda Thomas. *The International Dictionary of Quotations*. New York: Thomas Crowell, 1970.

Wright, John W., Ed. *The New York Times 1999 Almanac*. New York: Penguin Reference, 1998.